Home Made

Blessings

Cookbook

"...filling our hearts with food and gladness."

Acts 14:17

A Collection of Over 400 Recipes with Inspirational Phrases

By Diane Reasoner

Home Made Blessings

1st Printing March, 2003
7,500 copies
Printed in the United States of America

© Copyright 2002
Diane Reasoner, Atlanta, Georgia
All rights reserved.

ISBN 1-930170-07-6
Trademark #76/408666

Edited, Published and Manufactured in the United States of America.

P & P Publishing
3802 Antelope Trail
Temple, TX 76504

Cover and Book Design by
Laura Gomez, Atlanta, Georgia

Scripture from
The Holy Bible
King James Version

for additional copies
www.giftswithreason.com
or call 1-770-921-9181

Acknowledgments

There are so many people who have blessed my life that I cannot list them all. We often don't say 'thank you' enough to the people who mean so much to us. This book is in acknowledgment of those who have touched my life, even with the simplest of life's treasures. Their love and support have meant more to me than they will ever know. Thanks to all of the people who have given me recipes for this book. I cannot begin to name them all.

Thanks to my sister-in-law, Sharon, with whom this book would have never existed. To my friend and assistant, Jenny, who has so graciously enriched my life and supported me in this work. And, to my husband, who is my best friend and the love of my life. Through all of our life together, his love and support have never faded.

Introduction

On September 11, 2001, the United States suffered the loss of life, and endured threats to national security. For many of us it was a reality check. We stopped to think about the importance of our families and friends and what a blessing they are to our lives. We all need blessings, but too often we don't think about the ways we can bless the lives of those around us.

This book is written in the spirit of family. Think of it as a way for families to create their own 'homemade blessings' and as an opportunity to pass their blessings on to others. But you will find more than just recipes in this book. You'll find uplifting messages that strengthen, encourage, and maybe a little chuckle.

Enjoy the food; enjoy making it with your family, and look outside your home for others who may need a helping hand. Most of all, never forget to share your blessings with people around you.

About the Author

Elizabeth Diane Reasoner

Diane is a native of Sylacauga, Alabama, and currently resides in Atlanta. For the past fifteen years, she has worked in public relations and communications for the Georgia Baptist Convention in Atlanta, where she is currently director of Communications. She has earned a master of arts degree in human resources and a bachelor of science from Ottawa University in Kansas, as well as degrees from Florida Baptist College and Southwest Baptist University in Missouri.

Diane has received numerous awards and honors including Who's Who of American Women, 1993-94; International Who's Who of Professional and Business Women, 1990; and Outstanding Young Women of America, 1982; Southern Baptist Convention Christian Women of Excellence nominee, 1993; Florida Baptist College Outstanding Alumnus, 1995; Religious Communicators Council and Baptist Communicators Awards of Excellence and Merit, 1997-2001; National Printing Association Awards, 1996 and 1999. She has held membership in the National Organization of Female Executives, and Religious Public Relations Council. She is a member of Baptist Communicators Association where she has also served as vice president, 1994-95, and as president 2001-02. She has served Southern Baptists for 30 years in church, state, and national levels.

Diane is married to Dr. Richard Reasoner, founder and clinical director of Christian Counseling and Psychological Services, Inc. in Atlanta, Georgia. They are the proud parents of two sons, Richard Michael of Wells Real Estate Funds in Atlanta, and Robert Mark who is the owner operator of a Chick-fil-A store in Wake Forest, North Carolina. She has two daughters-in-law Karyn and Jennifer. The Reasoners are loving grandparents of Kole Zuba, born April 2002, and are expecting another grandchild in May 2003.

Foreword

Diane Reasoner has a job that requires her to attend many meetings and events where the participants share a meal. When you are responsible for public relations for a large religious organization, and you work constantly with church people, it is natural to become something of an authority on the subject of Christian hospitality.

Traditionally, church hospitality has centered around special meals, whether it be a formal banquet, church picnic, potluck supper, or food carried to shut-ins and the bereaved. When we read the gospels we find that many of the significant events in the life of Christ took place around the table, including The Last Supper. Food is not only one of life's necessities, it is also symbolic of Christian caring. It says that someone cares enough to take the time, and make the effort to prepare something special, and the food often reflects some measure of creativity on the part of the one who has prepared it.

This compilation of favorite recipes and pithy spiritual sayings comes from Diane's many friends throughout Georgia and the nation. You can be assured that the recipes have been tested over many special occasions shared by families and friends.

Perhaps there is no better place to find some gems of spiritual wisdom than in a cookbook. After all, cooking itself can be frustrating when you're out of the necessary ingredients, or time is running out, or the experimental dish is not turning out just as you had planned. At those times we may need some reminders that help us put things back in proper perspective.

Diane has also reminded us that as enjoyable as cooking and food may be, it takes on new meaning when we are able to share our bounty and culinary talents with family and friends. The gift of hospitality is alive and well within the pages of this "delicious" book.

Bill Neal, editor
The Christian Index

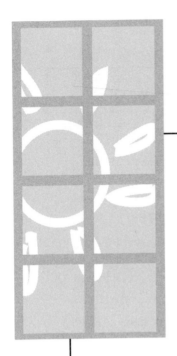

Table of Contents

In the
Beginning

BEVERAGES

SPREADS

DIPS

APPETIZERS

Living Happy Tea

1 cup friendly words

2 cups (heaping) understanding

1 cup discovery

8 tablespoons helpfulness

4 tablespoons (heaping) time

4 cups strength

10 tablespoons patience

1 cup loving attitude

2 pinches of warm personality

A dash of humor

LEMONADE SPICE TEA

2½ cups powdered orange drink
1 (0.23 ounce) package unsweetened lemonade
　soft drink mix
⅓ cup instant tea
2 cups sugar
2 teaspoons ground cinnamon
2 teaspoons ground cloves
½ teaspoon ginger

In a large container, combine all ingredients. Mix well. Add 2-3 tablespoons to 8 ounces hot water. Makes 6 servings.

SUNSHINE LEMONADE

1 cup sugar
5 cups cold water
1 cup lemon juice, approximately 6 lemons

In a large pitcher, dissolve sugar in one cup water and add lemon juice. Add remaining water and stir well. Serve over ice. Makes 6 servings.

APPLE HONEY TEA

1 (12 ounce) can frozen apple juice concentrate
2 tablespoons instant tea powder
1 tablespoon honey
½ teaspoon ground cinnamon

In a large beverage container, prepare apple juice concentrate according to package directions. Pour into crock-pot or slow cooker. Add tea, honey, and cinnamon. Stir to blend. Heat on low 1-2 hours. Stir well before serving. Makes 6 to 8 servings.

Nevertheless
He left
not himself
without witness,
in that He did good,
and gave us rain
from heaven, and
fruitful seasons,
filling our hearts
with food
and gladness.

Acts 14:17

FEAST PARTY PUNCH

1 cup sugar
1 cup hot water
2 (48 ounce) cans pineapple juice
1 (12 ounce) can frozen orange juice
1 (12 ounce) can frozen lemonade
1 (18 ounce) package whole strawberries
2 quarts ginger ale

In a large beverage container, dissolve sugar in hot water. Add pineapple juice, orange juice, lemonade, strawberries, and add ginger ale last. Chill and serve over a block of ice in a punch bowl. Makes 40 servings.

EVERGREEN PEPPERMINT PUNCH

2 cups sugar
2 quarts water
2 packages powdered drink mix (lime), unsweetened
1 (46 ounce) can pineapple juice
1 quart ginger ale
Peppermint extract to taste

In a large container, combine sugar, water, powdered drink mix, and pineapple juice. Chill. When ready to serve add ginger ale and peppermint extract. Makes 36 one-half cup servings.

Sometimes our light goes out but is blown into flame by an encounter with another human being. Each of us owes the deepest thanks to those who have rekindled this inner light.

Albert Schweitzer

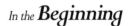
THIRST QUENCHER PUNCH

1 (14 ounce) can frozen lemonade, diluted
64 ounces pineapple juice
64 ounces pineapple-grapefruit juice
2 cups sugar
1 quart ginger ale

In a large container, combine lemonade, pineapple juice, pineapple-grapefruit juice, and sugar. Mix well. Pour punch into gallon containers. Freeze. Before serving, thaw five hours, then add ginger ale to each gallon of punch before serving. Punch will be "slushy", no ice will be needed. Makes 24 servings.

CRANBERRY SODA PUNCH

1 cup fresh orange juice
½ cup fresh lemon juice
16 ounces cranberry juice cocktail
1¼ cups sugar
4 cups chilled club soda
1 orange, sliced for garnish
1 lemon, sliced for garnish

In a large container, combine orange juice, lemon juice, cranberry juice cocktail, and sugar. Stir to dissolve sugar. Add club soda and pour over ice in a large pitcher. Garnish with orange and lemon slices. Makes 8 to 10 servings.

Those who decide
to use leisure
as a means of
mental development,
who love
the scriptures,
good friends,
good music,
good books,
good plays, and
good conversation—
what are they?
They are some of
the happiest people
in the world.

OPEN THOSE EYES
MORNING MILK SHAKE

cups milk
frozen bananas
tablespoons chocolate protein powder

n a blender, place all ingredients. Blend at high speed.
Makes 2 servings.

CHILLY VANILLA MILK SHAKE

½ teaspoon vanilla extract
cup chilled milk
heaping tablespoons vanilla ice cream

n a blender or milk shaker, combine all ingredients.
Blend until frothy. Pour into a tall glass and serve.
Makes 1 serving.

SAUCY CARAMEL SHAKE

tablespoons caramel sauce or topping
½ cup yogurt
½ cup chilled milk

n a blender or milk shaker, combine all ingredients.
Blend until thick and frothy. Pour into a tall glass and
erve immediately. Makes 1 serving.

Think not
of yourself
as the architect
of your career
but as the sculptor.
Expect to have to
do a lot of hard
hammering
and chiseling
and scraping
and polishing.

B. C. Forbes

SWEET CHILLED BANANA SHAKE

1 ripe banana, sliced
2 teaspoons sugar
2 ounces chilled milk
6 ounces chilled milk
3 heaping tablespoons vanilla ice cream

In a blender, place banana, sugar, and 2 ounces milk. Blend until smooth. Add 6 ounces milk and ice cream. Blend until mixture is thick and frothy. Pour into a tall glass and serve immediately. Makes 1 serving.

CANAAN FRUIT SHAKE

½ cup milk
½ cup orange juice
1 medium banana, sliced
3 heaping tablespoons vanilla ice cream

In a blender, combine all ingredients. Blend at medium speed. Pour into glasses and serve. immediately. Variations: use your favorite fruit. Makes 2 servings.

CREAMY SODA

1 tablespoon vanilla or maple syrup
4 heaping tablespoons vanilla ice cream
1 small bottle club soda or lemonade, chilled

In a tall glass, place vanilla or maple syrup, add ice cream. Gently fill glass with club soda or lemonade. Serve with long handled spoon and drinking straw. Makes 1 serving.

Homes are not built in isolation. Talk to your spouse and your children today about something that is important to them.

CHUG-A-LUG CHOCOLATE SODA

1 tablespoon chocolate topping or syrup
¼ cup milk
4 heaping tablespoons vanilla ice cream
1 small bottle club soda, chilled

In a tall glass, place chocolate topping or syrup and stir in milk. Add ice cream. Gently fill glass with club soda. Serve with a long handled spoon and drinking straw. Makes 1 serving.

CITY SLICKER STRAWBERRY SODA

1 tablespoon strawberry topping or syrup
¼ cup sliced fresh strawberries
2 heaping tablespoons strawberry ice cream
1 bottle club soda or lemonade, chilled
1 whole strawberry

In a tall glass, place the strawberry topping or syrup. Add strawberries and ice cream. Gently fill glass with chilled soda or lemonade. Serve with a long handled spoon and drinking straw. Garnish with one whole strawberry. Makes 1 serving.

PECAN ALE SODA

3 heaping tablespoons pecan ice cream
1 small bottle ginger ale, chilled
Mint sprigs

In a tall glass, place ice cream and top with ginger ale. Garnish with mint sprig, serve with drinking straw. Makes 1 serving.

Never lose an opportunity of seeing anything that is beautiful; for beauty is God's handwriting. Welcome it in every fair face, in every fair sky, in every fair flower, and thank God for it as a cup of blessing.

Ralph Waldo Emerson

FRUITY FROSTIES

1½ cups cold water
1 (10 ounce) package frozen strawberries, thawed
¾ cup frozen orange juice concentrate, thawed
1 ripe banana, sliced
1 cup ice cubes
8 fresh strawberries
8 orange slices

In a blender, combine water, thawed strawberries, orange juice concentrate, and banana pieces. Cover and blend or process until smooth. While blender is running, add ice cubes under lid, blend until mixture is smooth and slushy. Pour into glasses, garnish with whole strawberries and orange slices. Makes 8 servings.

SINLESS SMOOTHIE

Favorite fruit
1 cup fat-free custard style yogurt
  (your favorite flavor)
1 cup fat-free whipped topping

In a blender, combine all ingredients. Blend until smooth and creamy. Makes 2 servings.

DANDY ORANGE DRINK

1½ cups orange juice
½ cup tonic water
2 orange slices

Fill two glasses with ice. Pour ¾ cup orange juice into each glass, and top with ¼ cup tonic water. Stir. Garnish each glass with an orange slice. Makes 2 servings.

Having grandchildren is the best of all possible worlds. You can take them and have fun and then return them to their parents. They keep you young at heart.

YUMMY NUTMEG CIDER

(3 inch) cinnamon sticks
teaspoons whole cloves
teaspoon nutmeg
½ gallon apple cider
cup sugar
cups orange juice
½ cup lemon juice

ı cheesecloth, combine cinnamon sticks, cloves, and
utmeg. In a large saucepan, combine cheesecloth, apple
ider, and sugar. Mix well. Cover and simmer on low for 30
ınutes. Remove spices and stir in orange juice and lemon
ıice. Continue heating for 30 minutes. Makes 10 servings.

COMFORTING CRAN APPLE CIDER

½ gallon cranberry juice
½ gallon apple juice
¼ cup packed brown sugar
½ lemon, sliced
stick cinnamon
teaspoons whole cloves
teaspoons whole allspice

ı a large pan, pour cranberry and apple juices. Add sugar.
tir until dissolved. In a cheesecloth, place lemon slices,
innamon, cloves, and allspice. Add cheesecloth to juices.
immer together for twenty minutes. Serve hot. Makes
6 servings.

*Grandchildren
are God's
compensation
to us
for growing old.*

Anonymous

JONAH'S TUNA SPREAD

2 (6.2 ounce) cans tuna
½ cup cottage cheese
3 tablespoons lemon juice
½ teaspoon pepper

In a food processor, combine all ingredients. Blend until smooth. Serve with crackers or assorted vegetables. Makes 8 to 10 servings.

CRAB CHEESE SPREAD

1 (8 ounce) package cream cheese
1 cup mayonnaise
¾ cup flaked crab
¼ cup chopped green onions
¼ cup chopped red pepper
1 cup shredded Swiss cheese

Preheat oven to 325 degrees. In a large bowl, combine cream cheese, mayonnaise, crab, green onions, and red pepper. Mix well. Spread in a 9 inch pie pan. Sprinkle Swiss cheese on top of mixture. Bake for 30 minutes. Serve with crackers or toasted bread. Makes 20 servings.

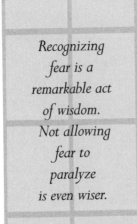

Recognizing fear is a remarkable act of wisdom. Not allowing fear to paralyze is even wiser.

SHRIMP BUTTER SPREAD

1 pound fresh shrimp, peeled, washed
  and deveined
2 teaspoons minced onion
3 tablespoons mayonnaise
2 (8 ounce) packages cream cheese
3 sticks butter

In a large bowl, chop shrimp into small pieces, reserving
a few for garnish. Blend in onion, mayonnaise, cream
cheese, and butter. Place whole shrimp on edge of bowl.
Chill and serve with crackers. Makes 20 servings.

PEPPER CHICKEN SPREAD

1 (8 ounce) package cream cheese
1 cup mayonnaise
1 (12.5 ounce) can white chicken, drained
¼ cup chopped green onions
¼ cup chopped red pepper
1 cup shredded Cheddar cheese

Preheat oven to 325 degrees. In a large bowl, combine
cream cheese, mayonnaise, chicken, onions, and pepper. In a
9 inch pie pan, spread mixture. Sprinkle Cheddar cheese on
top of mixture. Bake for 30 minutes. Serve with crackers.
Makes 12 to 14 servings.

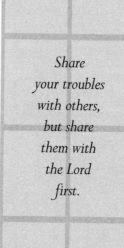

*Share
your troubles
with others,
but share
them with
the Lord
first.*

SAMSON'S SPINACH SPREAD

1 (10 ounce) package frozen chopped spinach,
   thawed
1 (1 ounce) envelope vegetable soup mix
1 cup sour cream

In a medium bowl, combine all ingredients. Mix well.
Serve with crackers. Makes 6 to 8 servings.

SEASONED VEGETABLE SPREAD

1 cup mayonnaise
1 cup sour cream
1½ teaspoons parsley flakes
1½ teaspoons onion powder or flakes
1½ teaspoons salad seasoning
1½ teaspoons dill weed

In a medium bowl, combine all ingredients. Mix well. Serve
with crackers. Makes 16 servings.

GARLIC FETA CHEESE SPREAD

4 ounces feta cheese, crumbled
1 (3 ounce) package cream cheese
⅓ cup mayonnaise
1 clove garlic, minced
¼ teaspoon dried basil
¼ teaspoon oregano
⅛ teaspoon dill
⅛ teaspoon thyme

In a large bowl, combine all ingredients. Mix well. Serve
with crackers. Makes 10 to 12 servings.

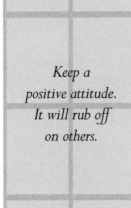

Keep a positive attitude. It will rub off on others.

CREAM CHEESE CRACKER SPREAD

2 (8 ounce) packages cream cheese
½ cup sour cream
1 cup finely chopped pecans

In a blender, combine all ingredients. Blend on a low speed until smooth. Makes 6 to 8 servings.

EVE'S BUTTER HIM UP SPREAD

4 pounds apples, peeled, cored, and sliced
2 teaspoons cinnamon
½ teaspoon ground cloves

In a slow cooker, place apples, cover and cook on high 2-3 hours. Reduce to low and cook 8 hours. Apples should be a rich brown. Stir in cinnamon and cloves. Cook on high 2-3 hours with lid off. Stir until smooth. Serve with crackers or toasted bread. Makes 15 servings.

CINNAMON PEACH SPREAD

4 (13 ounce) cans peaches, drained
2¾ cups sugar
2 teaspoons cinnamon
1 teaspoon ground cloves

In a blender, combine all ingredients. Blend until smooth and pour into slow cooker. Cover and cook on high 8-10 hours. Remove cover during last half of cooking time and stir occasionally. Serve with crackers or toasted bread. Makes 10 to 12 servings.

When a person talks about someone else's character they are really revealing their own.

STRAWBERRY ORANGE SPREAD

1 (8 ounce) package cream cheese
1 (10 ounce) jar strawberry jam or preserves
1 teaspoon dried orange peel
1 cup finely chopped pecans

In a large bowl, combine all ingredients. Mix well. Chill before serving. Serve with crackers or toasted bread. Makes 12 to 14 servings.

NUTTY CREAM CHEESE SPREAD

1 (8 ounce) package cream cheese
2 tablespoons butter, softened
2 tablespoons cream
½ tablespoon salt
¼ cup chopped pecans

In a large bowl, combine all ingredients. Mix well. Chill before serving. Serve with crackers or toasted bread. Makes 6 to 8 servings.

*Reconciliation
is more beautiful
than victory.*

Violeta Barrios de Chamorro

THICK FAT-FREE CHEESE DIP

(3 ounce) package fat-free cream cheese,
softened
½ cup fat-free sour cream
½ cup fat-free cottage cheese
tablespoon fat-free mayonnaise
teaspoons dried dill weed
½ teaspoon onion powder
½ teaspoon garlic powder
Raw vegetables or fat-free crackers

In a food processor or blender, combine all ingredients.
Blend until smooth. Serve with raw vegetables or fat-free
crackers. Makes 6 to 8 servings.

NO BEAN CHILI CHEESE DIP

(16 ounce) can chili with no beans
(10¾ ounce) can cheese soup
Chips

In a medium glass bowl, combine chili and soup. Microwave
on high for 2 to 3 minutes. Pour over chips. Makes 6 to 8
servings.

CHUNKY CHEESE DIP

(8 ounce) package cream cheese
cup shredded Mexican cheese
teaspoons milk
½ cup medium chunky style salsa
tortilla chips

In a medium saucepan, combine cream cheese and Mexican
cheese. Cook and stir over low heat until cheese is melted.
Add milk and salsa. Cook for 10 minutes until thoroughly
heated. Serve with tortilla chips. Makes 6 to 8 servings.

*Share
a smile with those
you love and
those you don't.*

HOT ONION DIP

1 cup finely chopped sweet onion
1 cup shredded Swiss cheese
1 cup mayonnaise

Preheat oven to 350 degrees. In a 9x13 inch baking pan, combine all ingredients. Mix well. Bake until bubbly. Serve with crackers. Makes 6 to 8 servings.

TWO STEP FRUITY DIP

1 (9 ounce) jar marshmallow créme
1 (8 ounce) package cream cheese, plain
**   or flavored**

In a medium bowl, combine marshmallow creme and cream cheese. Mix well. Serve with your favorite fruit. Makes 4 to 6 servings.

HOT STICKY APPLE DIP

½ cup butter
½ cup light corn syrup
1 cup packed brown sugar
1 (14 ounce) can sweetened condensed milk
Fresh apple slices

In a large saucepan, combine all ingredients. Mix well. Bring mixture to a boil. Pour mixture into a crock-pot. Set on low. Serve with fresh apple slices. Makes 15 servings.

There's always room for improvement — it's the biggest room in the house.

Louise Heath Leber

MISFIT FISH DIP

1 pint sour cream
1 pint French onion dip
2 (8 ounce) cans crab meat, washed and crumbled
1 (8 ounce) can shrimp, washed and chopped
½ teaspoon Worcestershire sauce
1 teaspoon lemon juice

In a large bowl, combine all ingredients. Mix well. Chill
for 2 hours before serving. Serve with crackers. Makes 20
servings.

CRAB IN CREAM DIP

1 cup mayonnaise
½ cup sour cream
1 tablespoon chopped parsley
1 (8 ounce) can crab meat
1 teaspoon lemon juice
Salt and pepper to taste
Crackers or raw vegetables

In a large bowl, combine all ingredients. Mix well. Serve
with crackers or raw vegetables. Makes 8 to10 servings.

*Let me give
so much time
to the improvement
of myself
that I won't
have any time
to criticize
others.*

TOMATO BACON CREAM DIP

1 medium tomato, diced
1 pound bacon, browned and crumbled
1½ teaspoons sour cream
1 cup mayonnaise
Toast wedges or raw vegetables

In a medium bowl, combine all ingredients. Mix well. Chill
before serving. Serve with toast wedges or raw vegetables.
Makes 10 to 12 servings.

ANYTIME VEGGIE DIP

1 pint mayonnaise
3 green onions, chopped
2 tablespoons fresh parsley
1 teaspoon lemon juice
Raw vegetables

In a medium bowl, combine all ingredients. Mix well. Chill before serving. Serve with raw vegetables. Makes 10 to 12 servings.

CHESTNUT DIP

1 pint sour cream
1 cup mayonnaise
1 (10 ounce) package frozen spinach, thawed, drained, and chopped
1 small onion, chopped
1 (8 ounce) can water chestnuts, sliced
1 (1 ounce) package vegetable soup mix
Raw vegetables or crackers

In a medium bowl, combine all ingredients. Mix well. Cover and chill before serving. Serve with raw vegetables or crackers. Makes 20 servings.

To attain excellence, you must care more than others think is wise, risk more than others think is safe, dream more than others think is practical.

Anonymous

BEEFY MEXICAN DIP

pounds Velveeta®
5 ounces hot or medium salsa
cup evaporated milk
pound ground beef, browned and crumbled
pound pork sausage, browned and crumbled
ortilla chips

a large saucepan, melt cheese. Add salsa and milk. Mix
ell. Add meats to cheese mixture. Serve hot with tortilla
hips. Makes 25 servings.

HABAÑERO AND LIME SALSA

(16 ounce) can Italian tomatoes
clove garlic, minced
small onion, chopped
bell pepper, chopped
habañero peppers, chopped
tablespoons fresh lime juice
alt and pepper to taste
tablespoon vegetable oil
ortilla chips

a food processor, combine all ingredients. Mix well.
over and chill before serving. Serve with tortilla chips.
lakes 10 to 12 servings.

*People become
stronger in the
face of adversity—
when we suffer
beyond the limits
of our own strength.*

NUTTY FRUIT TRAIL MIX

2 pounds dry roasted peanuts
2 pounds cashews
1 pound raisins
1 pound chocolate coated candy
½ pound flaked coconut

In a large bowl, combine all ingredients. Mix well.
Makes 50 servings.

HONEY PEANUT MIX

2 cups graham honey cereal
1 cup mini marshmallows
½ cup chocolate chips
1 cup peanuts
½ cup raisins

In a large bowl, combine all ingredients. Cover bowl and
shake well. Makes 10 to 12 servings.

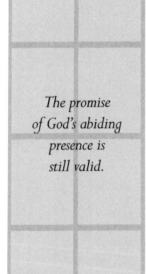

*The promise
of God's abiding
presence is
still valid.*

ALL SPICED-UP PECANS

1 egg white
½ teaspoon salt
2 cups pecan halves
½ cup sugar
1 teaspoon cinnamon
½ teaspoon allspice
¼ teaspoon ginger

Preheat oven to 350 degrees. In a medium bowl, combine
egg white and salt. Beat until frothy. Add pecans and stir
to coat. Drain excess liquid. In a large bowl, combine
sugar, cinnamon, allspice, and ginger. Coat nuts with sugar
mixture. Spread nuts onto ungreased baking sheet. Bake
for 20 minutes. Makes 6 to 8 servings.

SPINACH BALLS

2 (10 ounce) packages frozen chopped spinach
2 cups herb dressing mix
2 onions, grated
6 eggs, beaten
¼ cup buttermilk
½ cup grated Parmesan cheese
1 teaspoon salt
½ teaspoon pepper
Cooking spray

Preheat oven to 350 degrees. Prepare spinach according to package directions. Drain well. In a large bowl, place spinach, dressing mix, onions, eggs, buttermilk, Parmesan cheese, salt, and pepper. Mix well. Chill mixture and shape into balls. Spray a baking sheet with cooking spray and place balls. Bake for 20 minutes. Makes 24 servings.

MARINATED CARROTS

1 pound carrots, sliced in sticks
1 cup orange juice
2 tablespoons sugar

In a large bowl, combine all ingredients. Mix well. Marinate and chill for 2 hours. Remove from marinade. Makes 10 to 12 servings.

*We are only
as good as
our thoughts.*

29

TASTY DEVILED EGGS

6 hard boiled eggs, peeled
1/8 teaspoon mustard
3 1/2 tablespoons salad dressing
2 tablespoons sweet pickle relish
1/2 teaspoon salt
Pepper to taste

Cut eggs in halves, removing egg yolks. In a medium bowl combine yolks, mustard, salad dressing, relish, salt, and pepper. Fill egg white halves with mixture and serve. Makes 12 servings.

CRISP CHEESE CRACKERS

Cooking spray
1 cup self-rising flour
1 cup rice cereal
1 stick margarine
1/2 pound Cheddar cheese, shredded
1/4 cup finely chopped pecans
Red pepper to taste

Preheat oven to 450 degrees. Lightly coat a baking sheet with cooking spray. In a large bowl, combine all ingredients. Mix well. Form into balls. Place on prepared baking sheet and flatten with a fork. Bake 10 minutes. Makes 10 to 12 servings.

Watch out!
You might get
what you're after.

David Byrne

GRANDDADDY'S CHEESE BALL

(8 ounce) packages cream cheese
(3 ounce) packages sliced beef, chopped
bunch green onions, chopped
tablespoon Worcestershire sauce
½ cup chopped pecans

In a large bowl, combine cream cheese, beef, onions, and Worcestershire sauce. Mix well with hands and form a ball. In another large bowl, pour pecans. Roll cheese ball in pecans until well covered. Makes 20 servings.

TUNA CHEESE BALL

(6 ounce) cans tuna, drained
(8 ounce) package cream cheese
tablespoon lemon
tablespoons grated onion
cup chopped nuts

In a large bowl, combine all ingredients except nuts. Mix well. Roll in chopped nuts. Serve with crackers. Makes 16 to 18 servings.

ENGLISH MUFFIN PIZZA

English muffin, lightly toasted
tablespoons pizza sauce
¼ cup ground beef, browned and crumbled
½ cup shredded mozzarella cheese

Preheat oven to 300 degrees. Place muffin halves on baking sheet. Cover each half with sauce, meat, and cheese. Bake until cheese is lightly brown. Makes 1 serving.

*Though we travel
the world over
to find the beautiful,
we must carry it
with us or
we find it not.*

Ralph Waldo Emerson

SWEET ONION BEEF BALLS

1 pound ground beef
½ cup chopped sweet onion
2 tablespoons Worchester sauce
1 teaspoon salt
1 teaspoon pepper
½ teaspoon garlic salt
2 tablespoons packed brown sugar
2 cups mild barbeque sauce

In a large bowl, combine beef, onion, Worchester sauce, salt, pepper, garlic salt, and sugar. Roll into small balls. In a large saucepan, pour barbeque sauce and add balls. Cook on low heat for 1 hour. Makes 12 to 14 servings.

God's loving kindness continues and He gives food to every living thing.

MONTEREY AND SAUSAGE MUSHROOMS

½ pound Italian sausage
1 cup shredded Monterey Jack cheese
24 large mushrooms, stems removed, washed, drained, set caps aside
¼ cup salsa
¼ cup chopped green onions

Preheat oven to 350 degrees. In a large skillet, brown sausage and drain. Add cheese. Fill each mushroom cap with 1 teaspoon of sausage cheese mix. In a 15x10x1 inch baking pan, place mushrooms. Spoon salsa over mushrooms. Bake for 20 minutes. Sprinkle with green onions and serve. Makes 24 servings.

HAM AND CHEESE POPPERS

Cooking spray
1 loaf sliced bread, torn into pieces
ounces diced ham
ounces shredded American cheese
eggs, beaten
cup milk
Salt and pepper to taste

Preheat oven to 350 degrees. Coat mini-muffin pan with cooking spray. Tear bread into small pieces and place in muffin pan. Top bread with ham and cheese. In a small bowl, combine eggs and milk. Salt and pepper. Pour mixture over bread, ham, and cheese. Bake for 15 minutes. Makes 8 servings.

SAUCY WINGS

6 chicken wings
cup soy sauce
cups packed brown sugar

Preheat oven to 300 degrees. Place chicken wings in a Dutch oven. In a small bowl, combine soy sauce and brown sugar. Pour mixture over chicken. Cover and bake for 1 hour. Makes 18 servings.

*God may seem
late but he is
always on time.*

Anonymous

CHICKEN BACON TIDBITS

1 chicken breast, cooked
½ pound bacon

Preheat oven to broil. Cut chicken breast into bite-size pieces. Wrap each piece with bacon. Secure bacon with toothpicks. Place on a baking sheet and broil until bacon is crisp. Makes 8 to 10 servings.

ALMOND CHICKEN LOG

2 (8 ounce) packages cream cheese, softened
1 tablespoon bottled steak sauce
½ teaspoon curry powder
1½ cups chopped, cooked chicken
½ cup minced celery
¼ cup chopped parsley
¼ cup chopped, toasted almonds
Crackers

In a large bowl, combine cream cheese, steak sauce, and curry powder. Mix well. Blend in chicken, celery, and 2 tablespoons parsley. Refrigerate remaining parsley. Shape mixture into a 9 inch log. Wrap in plastic. Chill 4 hours or overnight. In a small bowl, combine remaining parsley and almonds and coat log. Serve with crackers. Makes 12 to 14 servings.

Find the recipe
for being happy.
Happiness
is not
found in things.
You can be
happy if your
heart is full
and your hands
are empty.

TURKEY TORTILLAS

¾ cup shredded Cheddar cheese
¾ cup shredded Monterey Jack cheese
1 pound ground turkey, browned and crumbled
1 (10¾ ounce) can tomato soup
1 cup salsa
½ cup milk
6 (6 inch) flour tortillas

Preheat oven to 400 degrees. In a medium bowl, combine Cheddar and Monterey Jack cheeses. In a large bowl, combine ½ of cheese mixture, turkey, soup, salsa, and milk. In a 2-quart shallow baking dish, pour mixture and bake for 30 minutes. Remove mixture from oven. Spoon mixture onto tortillas and roll. Cut rolls into bite-size pieces and top with remaining cheese mixture. Makes 8 to 10 servings.

TINY SHRIMP BALLS

1 (8 ounce) package cream cheese, softened
1 teaspoon dry mustard
½ teaspoon onion powder
1½ teaspoons lemon juice
⅛ teaspoon cayenne pepper
1½ cups frozen, cooked small shrimp,
    thawed and drained
Cocktail sauce

In a medium bowl, combine cream cheese, mustard, onion powder, lemon juice, and cayenne pepper. Fold in shrimp. Chill until slightly firm. Roll mixture into 1 inch balls. Place on serving platter. Refrigerate 45 to 60 minutes. Serve with toothpicks and dip in cocktail sauce, if desired. Makes 15 servings.

True and real
goodness is
not only
good for our life...
but it enriches
everyone
with whom we
come in contact.

SMOKED SALMON LOG

1 (16 ounce) can salmon, drained, boned, flaked
1 (8 ounce) package cream cheese
1 tablespoon lemon juice
2 teaspoons finely chopped onion
1 teaspoon Worcestershire sauce
¼ teaspoon salt
¼ teaspoon liquid smoke
Crackers

In a large bowl, combine all ingredients. Mix well. Form into a log and chill. Serve with crackers. Makes 30 servings.

KERNEL CRAB CAKES

Cooking spray
1 (8 ounce) can crab meat
2 tablespoons beaten egg
¼ cup bread crumbs
¼ cup frozen corn kernels
⅛ teaspoon cayenne pepper
⅛ teaspoon pepper
1½ teaspoons lemon juice
1 teaspoon Worcestershire sauce
1 tablespoon Dijon mustard
1 tablespoon sour cream

Preheat oven to 450 degrees. Lightly coat baking sheet with cooking spray. In a large bowl, combine all ingredients. Mix well. Roll mixture into balls and place on baking sheet. Flatten each ball with a spoon. Cover baking sheet with plastic wrap and chill until firm. Bake both sides 15 minutes, until lightly browned. Makes 15 servings.

*Do continue
to believe that
with your feeling
and your work
you are taking part
in the greatest;
the more strongly
you cultivate
in yourself
this belief,
the more will reality
and the world
go forth from it.*

Rainer Maria Rilke

Eden's Garden

Friendship

Fold two hands together
And express a dash of sorrow
Marinate it overnight
And work on it tomorrow.

Chop one grudge into tiny pieces
Add several cups of love.
Dredge with a large sized smile
Mix with the ingredients above.

Dissolve the hate within you,
By doing a good deed,
Cut in and help your friend,
If he should be in need.

Stir in laughter, love, and kindness
From the heart it has to come,
Toss with genuine forgiveness
And give your neighbor some.

The amount of people served
Will depend on you,
It can serve the whole wide world,
If you really want it to.

Anonymous

SOUPS

SALADS

ADAM'S CHOICE GARDEN VEGETABLE SOUP

Cooking spray
⅔ cup sliced carrots
½ cup diced onion
2 garlic cloves, minced
3 cups broth (beef, chicken, or vegetable)
1½ cups diced green cabbage
1 (14½ ounce) can green beans, drained
½ cup diced zucchini
1 tablespoon tomato paste
½ teaspoon dried oregano
2 teaspoons dried basil
¼ dried oregano
¼ teaspoon salt

Coat a large saucepan with cooking spray, sauté carrots, onion, and garlic over low heat until softened, about 5 minutes. Add broth, cabbage, beans, zucchini, tomato paste, oregano, basil, and salt. Bring to a boil. Cover and cook over low heat for 30 minutes. Makes 6 to 8 servings.

VEGETABLE BEAN SOUP

6 cups cooked beans: navy, pinto,
   and Great Northern
1 meaty ham bone
1 cup cooked, diced ham
¼ teaspoon garlic powder
1 small bay leaf
1 cup cubed potatoes
1 cup chopped onions
1 cup chopped celery
1 cup chopped carrots
3½ quarts water

In a large saucepan, combine all ingredients. Mix well. Cover and cook over medium heat for one hour. Remove bay leaf before serving. Makes 8 to 10 servings.

We all have an ugly section in our garden of life. God can help us transform that spot into something beautiful.

BLACK BEAN SOUP

cups chicken broth
(15 ounce) can black beans, drained
¼ cup diced carrots
1¼ cups chopped onions
⅓ cup diced celery
½ teaspoon oregano
½ teaspoon pepper
½ teaspoon garlic powder
cup diced potatoes

In a large soup pot, pour chicken broth. Heat over high heat. Combine beans, carrots, onions, celery, oregano, pepper, and garlic powder. Bring to a boil. Add potatoes. Cover and cook over low heat for 30 minutes. Makes 4 to 6 servings.

STICK-TO-YOUR RIBS VEGETABLE SOUP

cups water
(16 ounce) can Italian style tomatoes, finely chopped
(14½ ounce) can green beans, drained
(15¼ ounce) can white corn, drained
(10 ounce) can kidney beans, drained
cup frozen carrots
cup frozen peas
¼ cup finely chopped onions
cups pasta, cooked
teaspoon salt
¼ teaspoon Italian seasoning

In a large saucepan, combine all ingredients. Mix well. Cook over low heat for 35 minutes. Makes 6 to 8 servings.

With a little faith in yourself and the people around you, nothing is impossible.

SPLIT PEA SOUP

1 (12 ounce) bag dry split peas
1 pound sausage, browned and crumbled
6 cups water
2 medium potatoes, diced
1 onion, chopped
½ teaspoon dried marjoram, or thyme
½ teaspoon pepper

Wash and sort dried peas, removing any stones. In a slow cooker, combine all ingredients. Mix well. Cover and cook over low heat for 5 hours. Makes 6 to 8 servings.

CREAM OF BROCCOLI SOUP

1 small onion, chopped, sautéd
1 teaspoon oil
1 (16 ounce) package frozen broccoli
2 (10¾ ounce) cans cream of celery soup
1 (10¾ ounce) can cream of mushroom soup
1 cup shredded American cheese
20 ounces milk

In a large saucepan, combine all ingredients. Mix well. Cook over low heat for one hour. Makes 6 to 8 servings.

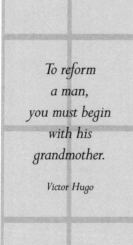

*To reform
a man,
you must begin
with his
grandmother.*

Victor Hugo

ALMOND POTATO SOUP

1 (10¾ ounce) can cream of potato soup
1½ soup cans of half and half cream
½ cup toasted, slivered almonds
1 (14 ounce) can chicken broth
¼ teaspoon salt
⅛ teaspoon pepper
Chives or parsley

In a blender, combine potato soup, cream, and almonds. Blend well. In a large saucepan, combine all ingredients. Cook over medium heat until soup is very hot, stirring occasionally. Garnish with chives or parsley. Makes 4 to 5 servings.

CREAMY POTATO SOUP

4½ cups water
½ cup cream of celery soup
½ cup chopped celery
3 medium potatoes, peeled and cubed
1½ teaspoons onion powder
1 cup milk
1 teaspoon salt

In a medium saucepan, combine all ingredients. Mix well. Bring to a boil. Cover and cook over low heat for 20 minutes, until vegetables are tender. Makes 4 servings.

Think of others first and you will forget your troubles.

MOZZARELLA ONION SOUP

2 cups thinly sliced onions
½ cup butter or margarine
¼ cup self-rising flour
1 (14 ounce) can chicken broth
2 cups milk
2 cups shredded mozzarella cheese

In a medium saucepan, cook onions in butter until tender over high heat. Stir in flour until blended. Gradually add broth and milk. Bring to a boil, stirring constantly for 1 minute. Over low heat, add cheese, and melt cheese (do not boil). Makes 6 to 8 servings.

NOT FEELIN' SO GOOD SOUP

1 (12½ ounce) can chicken
3 (14 ounce) cans chicken broth
8 ounces favorite noodles, uncooked
Salt and pepper to taste

In a large saucepan, combine all ingredients. Mix well. Cook over medium heat until noodles are tender. Salt and pepper. Makes 4 to 6 servings.

*Life paths
are made
for walking;
once the path
is traveled
it is easier to share
the directions
with others.*

Chicken Vegetable Noodle Soup

3¼ cups chicken broth
1 cup chopped onions
3 large carrots, peeled and sliced
2 celery stalks, sliced
1 large red bell pepper, chopped
1 pound chicken tenders, cubed
2 cups noodles, uncooked
¼ teaspoon pepper
¼ teaspoon garlic powder

In a large soup pot, pour ¼ cup chicken broth. Cook over medium high heat for 3 minutes. Add onions, carrots, celery, and red bell pepper. Cook 3 to 5 minutes, until tender-crisp. Pour remaining chicken broth into pot. Cook over high heat and bring soup to a boil. Add chicken pieces, noodles, pepper, and garlic powder. Cover and cook on low heat for 45 minutes. Makes 8 to 10 servings.

Turkey and Rice Soup

1 small onion, chopped
1 cup chopped celery
1 tablespoon oil
1 pound ground turkey, browned and crumbled
1 cup rice, cooked
1 (10¾ ounce) can cream of chicken soup
1 teaspoon salt

In a large saucepan, combine all ingredients. Mix well. Cover and cook over low heat for 45 minutes. Makes 4 to 6 servings.

Discipline is not a matter of technique; it is a matter of confidence.

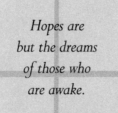

SOUTHERN BRUNSWICK SOUP

2 pounds pork
1 pound beef
2 quarts water
1 (16 ounce) can corn, drained
1 (16 ounce) can tomatoes
1 large onion, chopped
1 tablespoon Worcestershire sauce
2 tablespoons margarine
½ teaspoon red pepper
½ cup vinegar
1 (14 ounce) bottle ketchup
2 cups diced potatoes, cooked

In a large pot, pour water and boil meats until tender. Remove meat and slice finely. Place all ingredients back in large pot. Cover and cook for 1½ hours. Stir occasionally. Makes 6 to 8 servings.

Hopes are but the dreams of those who are awake.

Pindar

BEEF AND CABBAGE SOUP

1 pound ground beef, browned and crumbled
1 medium onion, chopped
1 (28 ounce) can tomatoes
2 cups water
1 (15 ounce) can kidney beans, drained
1 teaspoon salt
½ teaspoon pepper
1 tablespoon chili powder
½ cup chopped celery
2 cups cabbage, thinly sliced

Combine beef, onion, tomatoes, water, beans, salt, pepper, chili powder, and celery in slow cooker. Cover and cook over low heat 3 hours. Add cabbage. Uncover and cook over high heat 30-45 minutes longer. Makes 6 to 8 servings.

OUT ON THE RANGE SOUP

pound ground beef, browned and crumbled
(10¾ ounce) can vegetable soup
(10¾ ounce) can bean and bacon soup
(10¾ ounce) soup cans of water
(8 ounce) can tomato sauce
½ teaspoon chili powder
½ teaspoon sugar
½ teaspoon onion powder
teaspoon salt
½ teaspoon pepper

In a large pot, combine all ingredients. Mix well. Cover and
cook over low heat for 30 minutes. Makes 4 to 6 servings.

QUICK FIXIN' SOUP

pound ground beef, browned and crumbled
cups beef broth
cups tomato juice
(16 ounce) package frozen mixed vegetables
teaspoon salt

In a large pot, combine all ingredients. Mix well. Cover and
cook over low heat for 1 hour. Makes 4 to 6 servings.

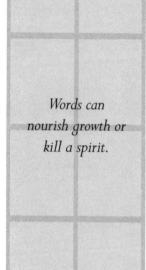

*Words can
nourish growth or
kill a spirit.*

SPICY VEGETABLE BEEF SOUP

1 pound ground beef
1 cup chopped onions
1 (30 ounce) jar meatless spaghetti sauce
3½ cups water
1 (16 ounce) package frozen mixed vegetables
1 (10 ounce) can diced tomatoes with green chiles
1 cup sliced celery
1 teaspoon beef bouillon granules
1 teaspoon pepper

In a large skillet, cook beef and onions until meat is no longer pink. Drain and place in a slow cooker. Stir in sauce, water, vegetables, chiles, celery, bouillon, and pepper. Cover and cook over low heat for 8 hours. Makes 6 to 8 servings.

CORN CHOWDER

6 slices bacon, browned and crumbled
½ cup chopped onions
2 cups peeled and diced potatoes
1 (10 ounce) package frozen corn
1 (14¾ ounce) can cream-style corn
1 tablespoon sugar
1 teaspoon Worcestershire sauce
1 teaspoon salt
¼ teaspoon pepper
1 cup water

In a large skillet, combine bacon, onions, and potatoes. Sauté for 5 minutes. Drain. In a large saucepan, combine all ingredients. Mix well. Cover and cook over low heat for 45 minutes. Makes 4 to 6 servings.

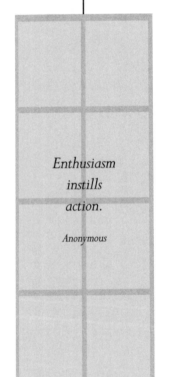

*Enthusiasm
instills
action.*

Anonymous

RICH AND EASY CLAM CHOWDER

(10¾ ounce) cans cream of potato soup
(10¾ ounce) cans New England clam chowder
½ cup butter
small onion, diced
pint half-and-half
(6½ ounce) cans clams, chopped

In a large saucepan, combine all ingredients. Mix well.
Cook over medium heat 45 minutes. Makes 4 to 6
servings.

SENSATIONAL CLAM CHOWDER

(14 ounce) can chicken broth
½ cup cream of celery soup, condensed
⅛ teaspoon pepper
3 cups diced potatoes
½ cup chopped celery
tablespoon onion powder
cup milk
2 tablespoons self-rising flour
2 (6½ ounce) cans minced clams

In a large saucepan, combine chicken broth, celery soup,
pepper, potatoes, celery, and onion powder. Bring to a boil
over high heat. Cover and cook over low heat. Simmer 15
to 20 minutes, until vegetables are tender. In a small bowl,
combine milk with flour. Mix until smooth. Gradually add
milk and flour to broth, stir to avoid lumps. Cook until
mixture starts to thicken. Stir in clams. Increase heat to
medium high and bring to a boil. Reduce heat to medium.
Stir constantly, until soup is thick and heated thoroughly.
Makes 4 to 6 servings.

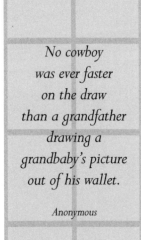

*No cowboy
was ever faster
on the draw
than a grandfather
drawing a
grandbaby's picture
out of his wallet.*

Anonymous

GARDEN OF EDEN SUMMER SALAD

7 cups mixed lettuce greens
1 tablespoon vinegar
1 teaspoon Dijon mustard
1 tablespoon extra virgin olive oil
1 cup sliced cucumber
1 cup sliced radishes
1 cup sliced mushrooms
Vinegar

Rinse lettuce and dry on paper towels (or salad spinner). In a small bowl, whisk together vinegar and mustard until smooth, then whisk in olive oil. In a large bowl, place lettuce, cucumbers, radishes, and mushrooms. Pour in mustard, oil, and vinegar mixture and gently toss salad to coat. Mix well and chill. Makes 6 to 8 servings.

*God
is faithful
even when
we are not.*

MIXED GREEN SALAD WITH ARTICHOKES

1 (6 ounce) jar marinated artichoke hearts
2 tablespoons mayonnaise
6 cups torn, mixed salad greens
16 red or yellow cherry tomatoes, halved
Toasted sesame seeds, optional

Drain artichokes, reserving 2 tablespoons of liquid. Cut artichokes into bite-size pieces. In a small bowl, place mayonnaise. Stir in artichoke liquid. Mix well. In a large bowl, mix greens, artichokes, and cherry tomatoes. Combine mayonnaise mixture. Mix well. Sprinkle with sesame seeds. Makes 4 to 6 servings.

FIRE AND ICE SALAD

2 large purple onions, cut in ¼ inch slices
5 large, firm tomatoes, peeled and quartered
1 bell pepper, seeded and cut into strips
¼ cup cider vinegar
¼ cup water
1½ teaspoons celery seed
1½ tablespoons mustard seed
½ teaspoon salt
2 tablespoons sugar
½ teaspoon cracked black pepper

In a large bowl, place onions, tomatoes, and bell pepper. In a large saucepan, place vinegar, water, celery seed, mustard seed, salt, sugar, and pepper. Bring to a boil for 1 minute. Pour liquid over vegetables and chill. Makes 6 servings.

ITALIAN BREAD SALAD

5 cups cubed day-old Italian bread
2 cups chopped tomatoes
1 cup fresh, cubed mozzarella cheese
½ teaspoon basil
¼ cup thinly sliced green onions
½ cup bottled red wine vinaigrette salad dressing

In a large bowl, combine bread, tomatoes, cheese, basil, and onions. Drizzle vinaigrette over salad. Toss lightly to coat. Makes 2 to 4 servings.

*He is a
great observer,
and He looks
quietly through
the deeds
of men.*

William Shakespeare

CRUNCHY, CRISP CHEESE SALAD

1 head fresh radicchio
2 bunches watercress
2 ounces Danish blue cheese
⅛ cup balsamic vinaigrette
2 tablespoons dry, roasted sunflower seeds

Wash, dry, and trim radicchio and watercress. Remove any leaves that are yellowing or tough. In a large bowl, combine radicchio and watercress. Mix well. Crumble cheese over greens. Pour vinaigrette over salad and toss until all leaves are well-coated with vinaigrette. Top salad with sunflower seeds. Makes 8 servings.

CAESAR SALAD

½ cup olive oil
3 anchovy fillets, optional
2 tablespoons lemon juice
1 teaspoon Worcestershire sauce
1 clove garlic, halved
10 cups torn romaine leaves
1 cup prepared garlic flavored croutons
¼ cup shredded Parmesan cheese
Coarse ground black pepper, to taste

In a blender, combine oil, fillets, lemon juice, Worcestershire sauce, and garlic. Blend until smooth. Cover and chill. In a large bowl, combine romaine, croutons, and cheese. Pour blended mixture over salad. Mix well. Season with pepper to taste. Makes 6 to 8 servings.

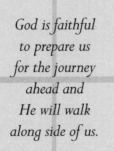

*God is faithful
to prepare us
for the journey
ahead and
He will walk
along side of us.*

ITALIAN TOMATO SALAD

1 tablespoon white wine vinegar
5 tablespoons olive oil
¼ teaspoon dried oregano
4 large tomatoes, sliced
¼ cup sliced black olives
½ pound fresh mozzarella cheese, sliced
12 fresh basil leaves
Salt and pepper to taste

In a small bowl, combine vinegar, olive oil, and dried oregano. On a serving plate, place tomatoes and black olives. Top with cheese, and cover with vinegar dressing. Garnish with basil leaves. Salt and pepper. Makes 4 to 6 servings.

SOUTHERN POTATO SALAD

6 eggs, boiled and chopped
5 large potatoes, boiled, cut into bite-size pieces
2 tablespoons sweet pickles
1 medium apple, chopped
1 teaspoon mustard
¼ teaspoon salt
1 small onion, chopped
4 tablespoons mayonnaise or salad dressing

In a large bowl, combine all ingredients. Mix well. Makes 8 to 10 servings.

*Too many people
use religion
like a spare tire,
only in emergencies.*

Anonymous

RICE SALAD

3 cups cooked rice
¼ cup chopped chives
1 cup grated carrots
1½ cups English peas, cooked and drained
¼ cup diced pimientos
1 cup diced Cheddar cheese
1 tablespoon dry Italian salad dressing mix
¾ cup mayonnaise

In a large bowl, combine rice, chives, carrots, peas, pimientos, and cheese. In a small bowl, blend dressing and mayonnaise. Combine dressing and rice mixture. Toss lightly. Chill. Makes 4 servings.

Focusing on hope during difficult times proves to be a challenge, but hope sometimes is all we have.

BROCCOLI SALAD

1 head broccoli, trimmed and cut into
   bite-size pieces
8 slices cooked bacon, cooked crisp and crumbled
¼ cup chopped onions
½ cup raisins
1 cup mayonnaise
2 tablespoons vinegar
¼ cup sugar

In a large bowl, combine broccoli, bacon, onions, and raisins. In a small bowl, combine mayonnaise, vinegar, and sugar. Mix well. Pour mixture over broccoli and toss gently. Makes 6 servings.

CAULIFLOWER SALAD

1 cauliflower head, separated into small flowerets
½ cup chopped bell pepper
2 medium tomatoes, chopped
¼ cup chopped green onions
⅔ cup sour cream
3 tablespoons mayonnaise
1 teaspoon dry mustard
1 teaspoon sugar
1 teaspoon dried dill weed

In a large bowl, combine cauliflower, pepper, tomatoes, and onions. In a medium bowl, combine sour cream, mayonnaise, mustard, sugar, and dill. Mix well. Combine all ingredients and toss. Makes 6 to 8 servings.

LONGLASTING SLAW

1 tablespoon salt
1 cup vinegar
1 cup water
1¾ cups sugar
2 teaspoons celery seed
2 heads cabbage, shredded
1 green pepper

In a medium saucepan, combine salt, vinegar, water, sugar, and celery seed. Cook over medium heat until sugar is melted. Cool at room temperature. In a large bowl, combine cabbage, pepper, and vinegar mixture. Store covered and chill. It will keep for two weeks. Makes 8 to 10 servings.

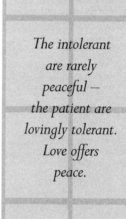

*The intolerant
are rarely
peaceful —
the patient are
lovingly tolerant.
Love offers
peace.*

CHINESE SLAW

4 cups shredded cabbage
¾ cups shredded carrots
¼ cup vegetable oil
¼ cup cider vinegar
3 tablespoons sugar
¼ teaspoon ginger powder
⅛ teaspoon red or black pepper

In a large bowl, combine cabbage and carrots. In a medium saucepan, combine oil, vinegar, sugar, ginger, and pepper. Cover and cook over low heat until sugar is dissolved. Pour mixture over cabbage and carrots. Toss well. Chill. Makes 4 to 6 servings.

SPICY STEAMY BEAN SALAD

1 (14½ ounce) can green beans, drained
1 teaspoon garlic or onion powder
1 (1 ounce) package Italian dressing

In a steamer, steam beans until crisp-tender. Sprinkle with onion or garlic powder, and dressing. Mix well and chill. Makes 2 servings.

*How can you
expect to love
someone and not
feel pain
when they die?
For God to
take away
our pain,
He would have
to take away
our feelings
and memories also.*

THREE BEAN SALAD

1 cup drained green beans
1 cup drained wax beans
1 cup drained kidney beans
1/2 cup chopped green pepper
1/2 cup minced onion
1/2 cup salad oil
1/2 cup vinegar
1/2 cup sugar
1 teaspoon salt

In a large bowl, combine all beans. Mix well. In a medium size bowl, combine green pepper, onion, oil, vinegar, sugar, and salt. Pour ingredients over beans. Mix well and chill. Makes 6 servings.

VEGGIE SALAD

1 (14½ ounce) can French green beans, drained
1 (15 ounce) can whole kernel corn, drained
1 onion, chopped
1 green pepper, chopped
1 red sweet pepper, chopped
2 stalks celery, chopped
1 cup sugar
1/3 cup vinegar
1/2 cup salad oil
2 teaspoons salt

In a large bowl, combine all ingredients. Mix well and chill. Makes 6 to 8 servings.

You can pour syrup on a bad experience, but it will still taste bad.

FROZEN FRUIT SALAD

1 (6 ounce) can frozen orange juice
1 (6 ounce) can frozen lemonade
1 (16 ounce) package frozen strawberries
1 (10 ounce) package frozen red raspberries
1 (16 ounce) package frozen blackberries
1 (20 ounce) can pineapple chunks, with juice
1 (29 ounce) can peaches, sliced and cut up,
   with juice
5 bananas, sliced
1¼ cups sugar
2 cups water
½ cup apricot nectarine juice

Thaw all of the frozen fruit and juice. In a large container, combine all ingredients. Mix well. Spoon mixture into cup cake holders and freeze. Partially thaw to serve. Makes 12 to 14 servings.

FRUITY COCONUT SALAD

1 (20 ounce) can pineapple chunks, drained
1 (11 ounce) can mandarin orange sections,
   drained
1 or 2 apples, chopped
1½ cups seedless grapes
1 cup miniature marshmallows
1 cup flaked coconut
1 cup chopped pecans
1 cup dairy sour cream
1 or 2 tablespoons sugar

In a large bowl, combine pineapple, orange sections, apples, grapes, marshmallows, coconut, and nuts. In a small bowl, combine sour cream and sugar. Stir into fruit mixture. Mix well and chill. Makes 8 to 10 servings.

*A smile is a curve
that can set
things straight.*

Anonymous

TIDBIT FRUIT SALAD

3 apples, cored and cubed
½ pound seedless grapes
1 banana, thinly sliced
1 celery stalk, finely chopped
1 (8 ounce) can pineapple tidbits, drained
¼ cup chopped walnuts
1 tablespoon honey
1½ cups vanilla yogurt

In a large bowl, combine all ingredients. Mix well and chill.
Makes 4 to 6 servings.

DICED RED DELICIOUS APPLE SALAD

4 cups diced Red Delicious apples
1½ cups halved seedless green grapes
½ cup finely chopped celery
½ cup finely shredded carrots
3 tablespoons fresh lemon juice
¼ cup plain fat-free yogurt
3 tablespoons honey
¼ cup finely chopped pecans
1 ounce blue cheese, crumbled

In a large bowl, combine apples, grapes, celery, carrots,
and lemon juice. Mix well. In a small bowl, combine yogurt
and honey. Mix well. Pour yogurt and honey over apple
mixture. Toss gently to coat. Sprinkle with pecans and
cheese. Make 6 to 8 servings.

*Plan ahead —
it wasn't raining
when Noah
built the ark.*

Anonymous

WALDORF SALAD

1 cup chopped apples
¼ cup chopped celery
2 tablespoons mayonnaise
½ cup finely chopped pecans

In a large bowl, combine all ingredients. Mix well. Serve chilled. Makes 2 servings.

SPINACH SALAD WITH CHERRIES

¼ cup olive oil
¼ cup red wine vinegar
2 teaspoons honey
⅛ teaspoon black pepper
10 spinach leaves, stems removed
1 cup fresh pineapple wedges
½ cup dried tart cherries
½ cup thinly sliced red onions
½ cup crumbled feta cheese

In a small bowl, combine oil, vinegar, honey, and pepper. Mix well. In a large bowl, combine spinach, pineapple, cherries, and onions. Add vinegar mixture. Mix well and top with cheese. Makes 4 to 6 servings.

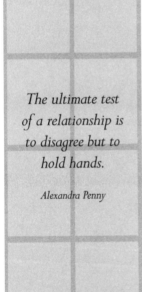

The ultimate test of a relationship is to disagree but to hold hands.

Alexandra Penny

Big Strawberry Salad

1 (6 ounce) package strawberry flavored gelatin
1 (8¼ ounce) can crushed pineapple
1 (21 ounce) can strawberry pie filling
3 cups boiling water

In a 9x13 glass pan, combine all ingredients. Mix well. Chill until set.

Icing

8 ounces sour cream
8 ounces cream cheese
½ cup sugar
1 teaspoon vanilla
½ cup chopped nuts

In a medium bowl, combine all ingredients. Mix well. Spread mixture on top of the gelatin mixture. Chill until set. You may choose other fruits. Makes 6 to 8 servings.

Cherry Berry Salad

1 (3 ounce) package cherry gelatin
1¼ cups boiling water
1 (16 ounce) can whole cranberry sauce
¼ teaspoon salt
¼ cup chopped pecans
¼ cup diced celery
1 cup sour cream

In a medium bowl, place gelatin and dissolve with water. Chill until slightly firm. In a small mixing bowl, add cranberry sauce and salt. Break up cranberry sauce with a fork. Add pecans and celery into gelatin. Mix well. Fold in sour cream. Refrigerate until set firmly. Makes 4 to 6 servings.

Children are called offspring for a reason. Build your marriage so you will know who you are married to when your children leave home.

Richard Reasoner

SUMMER TIME MELON SALAD

1 (6 ounce) can frozen lemonade concentrate, thawed
¼ cup orange marmalade
2 tablespoons orange juice
2 cups assorted melon balls
  (cantaloupe, honeydew, watermelon)
½ cup halved strawberries
1 small pineapple, peeled, cored, and cubed
3 small cantaloupes, halved and seeded
Sprig of mint

In a large bowl, combine lemonade, marmalade, and orange juice. In a large bowl, place melon balls, strawberries, and pineapple. Pour lemonade mixture over fruit, stirring gently. Cover and chill at least 2 hours. Spoon fruit mixture into cantaloupe halves. Garnish with mint, if desired. Makes 6 servings.

BLUEBERRY SALAD

2 (3 ounce) packages raspberry gelatin
1 (8 ounce) can crushed pineapple with juice
1 cup blueberry pie filling
1 (8 ounce) package cream cheese, softened
½ pint sour cream
½ cup sugar
½ teaspoon vanilla
1 cup chopped, toasted pecans

In a 9x13 inch baking pan, mix gelatin according to package directions. Combine gelatin, pineapple, and blueberry filling and congeal. In a large bowl, combine cream cheese, sour cream, sugar, and vanilla. Mix well. Spread cream mixture over congealed mixture. Sprinkle with toasted pecans. Cut in squares. Makes 6 to 8 servings.

*Love
is unconditional.
The love of Christ
can live in you
and be shared
with others as
you go about
your life today.*

FLUFFY FRUIT SALAD

2 (20 ounce) cans crushed pineapple
⅔ cup sugar
2 tablespoons all-purpose flour
2 eggs, lightly beaten
¼ cup orange juice
3 tablespoons fresh lemon juice
1 tablespoon vegetable oil
2 (17 ounce) cans fruit cocktail, drained
2 (11 ounce) cans mandarine oranges, drained
2 bananas, sliced
1 cup heavy cream, whipped

In a large saucepan, drain pineapple juice, reserving 1 cup juice, place juice in saucepan. Combine juice, sugar, flour, eggs, orange juice, lemon juice, and oil. Bring to a boil, stirring constantly. Boil for 1 minute. Remove from heat and cool. In a large bowl, combine pineapple, fruit cocktail, oranges, and bananas. Fold in whipped cream. Chill for several hours. Makes 18 to 20 servings.

AMBROSIA SALAD

1 (3 ounce) package orange gelatin
½ cup sugar
1 (8 ounce) can crushed pineapple with juice
1 cup flaked coconut
1 cup chopped pecans
1 cup sour cream
3 oranges, cut in bite-sizes

In a large bowl, mix gelatin according to package directions. Add sugar. Dissolve until thickened. Combine pineapple, coconut, pecans, sour cream, and oranges. Chill. Makes 6 to 8 servings.

Home is the only place where, when you have to go there they have to take you in.

Robert Frost

CREAMY ORANGE SALAD

1 (3 ounce) package orange gelatin
½ cup sugar
1 cup boiling water
½ pint sour cream
1 (11 ounce) can mandarin oranges, drained
1 (8 ounce) can crushed pineapple

In large bowl, dissolve gelatin and sugar in boiling water. Cool slightly. Blend in sour cream. Add mandarin oranges and pineapple. Chill until firm. Makes 4 to 6 servings.

PINEAPPLE SALAD

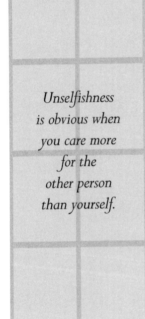

*Unselfishness
is obvious when
you care more
for the
other person
than yourself.*

1 (8 ounce) can crushed pineapple
1 cup water
1 (3 ounce) box lemon or orange gelatin
1 cup shredded mild Cheddar cheese
¾ cup salad dressing
1 (5 ounce) can evaporated milk
½ cup chopped pecans or walnuts

In a measuring cup, drain juice from pineapple and add enough water to make 1 cup. In a small saucepan, pour the liquid and bring to a boil. In a small mixing bowl, place gelatin and pour the liquid over the gelatin. Stir to dissolve the gelatin and allow to cool for a few minutes. Add one additional cup of water. Stir in the crushed pineapple, cheese, salad dressing, milk, and nuts. Chill until firm and serve. Makes 4 to 6 servings.

CLASSIC WATERCRESS SALAD

1 bunch watercress, washed,
   dried and pulled apart
1 pound tomatoes, chopped
1 (8 ounce) package cream cheese,
   cut in bite-size pieces
1 small bunch chives
2 tablespoons fresh thyme
⅛ teaspoon pepper
½ teaspoon sugar
½ teaspoon powdered mustard
2 tablespoons cider vinegar
1½ tablespoons olive oil

In a large bowl, combine watercress, tomatoes, cheese, chives, and thyme. In a blender, combine pepper, sugar, mustard, vinegar, and oil. Blend. Pour over salad and toss lightly. Makes 6 to 8 servings.

VEGGIE PASTA SALAD

6 ounces corkscrew pasta, cooked and drained
1 (14½ ounce) can green beans, drained
1 (11 ounce) can whole kernel corn, drained
1 (8¼ ounce) can sliced carrots, drained
1 (2½ ounce) can ripe olives, drained
1 cup Italian dressing
⅓ cup sliced green onions
⅓ cup diced red or green pepper
Romaine lettuce

In a large bowl, combine pasta, beans, corn, carrots, olives, dressing, onions, and pepper. Mix well. Chill. Divide lettuce leaves onto 6 to 8 plates. Spoon mixture onto lettuce leaves. Makes 6 to 8 servings.

Turn an obstacle into an opportunity.

VERMICELLI SALAD

1 (12 ounce) package vermicelli,
   cooked and drained
4 tablespoons oil
3 tablespoons lemon juice
1 clove garlic
1 cup chopped celery
1 cup chopped bell pepper
1 cup chopped black olives
½ cup chopped onion
Mayonnaise

In a large bowl, combine vermicelli, oil, lemon juice, and garlic. Toss and chill. Add celery, bell pepper, olives, and onions. Mix well. Add mayonnaise and chill. Makes 4 to 6 servings.

HAM AND PASTA SALAD

2 cups cooked and drained rotini macaroni
1½ cups chopped tomatoes
1 cup shredded yellow summer squash
2 ounces cooked ham
¼ cup snipped fresh basil
⅓ cup bottled balsamic vinaigrette salad dressing
12 thin slices cantaloupe

In a large bowl, combine pasta, tomatoes, squash, ham, and basil. Pour salad dressing over salad. Toss lightly to coat. To serve, fan 3 slices of cantaloupe on 4 plates and top with salad. Makes 4 servings.

*A happy family
is but an
earlier heaven.*

Anonymous

PASTA CHICKEN SALAD

(12½ ounce) can white chicken
(16 ounce) box macaroni, cooked and drained
tablespoons salad dressing
lettuce leaves
2 small sweet pickles
boiled eggs, sliced
tomatoes, sliced

In a large bowl, combine chicken, macaroni, and salad dressing. Mix well. Chill. Divide lettuce leaves onto 6 plates. Spoon mixture onto lettuce leaves. Garnish with pickles, eggs, and tomatoes around the plate. Makes 6 servings.

LAZY CHICKEN SALAD

cups cooked, cubed chicken
½ pound white seedless grapes
ounces water chestnuts, sliced
½ cup chopped celery
(6 ounce) can pineapple tidbits, drained
½ cup toasted almond slivers
large lettuce leaves

In a large bowl, combine chicken, grapes, chestnuts, celery, pineapple, and almond slivers. Mix well.

DRESSING

¼ cup mayonnaise
½ teaspoon curry powder
½ tablespoon lemon juice

In a small bowl, combine all ingredients. Mix well. Pour dressing over salad. Mix well and chill. Divide lettuce leaves onto 4 plates. Spoon mixture onto lettuce leaves. Makes 4 servings.

Trouble spots in a relationship do not need to become a permanent separation.

SAUCY CHICKEN MELON SALAD

1 pound cooked chicken breast, cubed
1 small honeydew melon, cubed
¼ cup honey
¼ cup lemon juice
1 tablespoon grated fresh ginger

In a large bowl, place chicken and melon. In a small bowl, combine honey, lemon juice, and ginger. Pour over chicken and melon. Toss gently. Makes 4 servings.

COOL AS A CUCUMBER CHICKEN SALAD

3 boneless cooked chicken breasts, sliced
8 medium cucumbers, with skin, sliced
1 red Spanish onion, sliced ½"
1 (32 ounce) bottle olive oil and vinegar dressing
4 teaspoons dry dill weed
2 teaspoons minced, dry parsley
6 lettuce leaves
½ cup chopped pecans

In a large non-metal bowl, combine all ingredients, but lettuce. Mix well. Chill and marinate over night before serving. Divide lettuce leaves onto 6 plates. Spoon mixture onto lettuce leaves. Top with pecans. Makes 6 servings.

*Make sure
the argument
is worth the fight
before you
start one.*

PIZZA IN A BOWL

¾ cup bottled western or French salad dressing
1 tablespoon snipped fresh basil or oregano
8 cups torn romaine
1 (8 ounce) package Italian bread shells,
    torn into bite-size pieces
1 cup chopped Canadian style bacon or pepperoni
1 cup shredded mozzarella cheese

In a small bowl, combine salad dressing and basil or oregano. Mix well. In an extra-large bowl, combine romaine, bread shells, bacon or pepperoni, and cheese. Drizzle with dressing. Toss until coated. Makes 4 to 6 servings.

TACO SALAD

1 pound ground beef, browned,
    crumbled and drained
1 head lettuce, shredded
1 red onion, chopped
1 cup shredded Cheddar cheese
1 (19 ounce) can kidney beans
½ cup Thousand Island dressing
12 ounces salsa
1 (13½ ounce) bag tortilla chips

In a large bowl, combine ground beef, lettuce, onion, cheese, beans, dressing, and salsa. Mix well. Place chips in a bowl and place mixture on top of chips. Makes 4 to 6 servings.

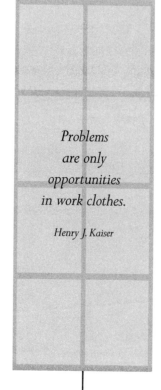

*Problems
are only
opportunities
in work clothes.*

Henry J. Kaiser

BEEFY APPLE SALAD

¼ cup apple juice
¼ cup salad oil
2 tablespoons wine vinegar
8 lettuce leaves
2 medium apples or pears, cut into wedges
½ pound lean cooked beef,
    cut into thin bite-size strips
2 medium carrots, cut into bite-size strips
¼ cup dried cherries or cranberries
½ teaspoon coarsely ground black pepper

In a screw-top jar, combine apple juice, salad oil, and vinegar. Cover and shake well. Divide lettuce leaves onto 4 plates. Arrange the apples, beef, and carrots on top of lettuce. Top with cherries. Drizzle dressing over salads and sprinkle with pepper. Makes 4 servings.

BALSAMIC-GLAZED LAMB SALAD

1 cup balsamic vinegar
6 cups torn mixed salad greens
8 lamb loin chops, cooked, cut into bite-size strips
3 cups sugar snap peas, ends trimmed
¼ cup hazelnuts or walnuts

In a small saucepan, pour vinegar. Boil gently, uncovered, until vinegar is reduced to ⅓ cup. Divide salad greens among 4 plates. Top with lamb and peas. Drizzle with glaze and sprinkle with nuts. Makes 4 servings.

A wise son accepts his father's discipline and will grow to love his father.

SWEET POTATO SAUSAGE SALAD

1 pound sweet potatoes or yams,
  peeled and cut into ½ inch pieces
1 small onion, cut into thin wedges
2 tablespoons margarine or butter
1 pound cooked smoked sausage,
  cut diagonally into ½ inch thick slices
2 medium cooking apples, cut into wedges
¼ teaspoon brown sugar
½ cup bottled sweet-and-sour sauce
½ teaspoon caraway seed
6 cups torn fresh spinach

In a large skillet, cook potatoes and onions in margarine
or butter over medium heat about 10 minutes, stirring
occasionally. Stir in sausage, apples, brown sugar, sweet-and-
sour sauce, and caraway seed. Cook, covered, over medium
heat about 3 minutes or until apples are tender and sausage
is heated thoroughly, stirring occasionally. Divide spinach
among 4 plates. Place cooked mixture over spinach. Makes
4 servings.

BLUE CHEESE, HAM
AND FRUIT SALAD

1 (8 ounce) package bow-tie pasta, cooked
1 papaya or mango, seeded, peeled,
  and cut into bite-size chunks
1 cup pineapple chunks
¼ pound ham, cut into bite-size chunks
½ cup chopped red pepper
½ cup chopped green onions
½ cup bottled blue cheese salad dressing
2 tablespoons snipped, fresh cilantro

In a large bowl, combine pasta, papaya or mango, pineapple,
ham, pepper, and green onions. Pour salad dressing over
salad. Toss lightly to coat. Sprinkle with cilantro. Makes
4 servings.

*Both in thought
and in feeling,
even though
time is real,
to realize the
unimportance
of time
is the gate
of wisdom.*

Bertrand Russell

CURRIED CRAB SALAD

2 cups cut up fresh fruit (such as pineapple,
  cantaloupe, honeydew or strawberries)
1 (6 ounce) package crab meat
¾ cup sliced celery
¼ cup light mayonnaise or salad dressing
¼ cup plain yogurt
2 tablespoons milk
½ teaspoon curry powder
4 cups torn mixed salad greens
Fresh raspberries (optional)

In a large bowl combine fresh fruit, crab meat, and celery.
In a medium bowl, combine mayonnaise or dressing,
yogurt, milk, and curry powder. Divide salad greens among
3 plates. Top with crab mixture and drizzle with dressing.
If desired, sprinkle with raspberries. Makes 3 servings.

CRAB CAESAR SALAD

1 (8 ounce) package crab meat
1 (12 ounce) package pre-cut lettuce
½ cup croutons
1 (8 ounce) bottle Caesar dressing
¼ cup Parmesan cheese

In a large bowl, combine crab meat, lettuce, croutons, and
dressing. Top with cheese. Makes 4 servings.

*Let there come
to me a
quietness of soul,
a relaxed body,
an alert mind,
a gentle touch,
and inner peace,
and integrity
of being.*

Kenneth Chafin

TUNA TWO BEAN SALAD

1 cup macaroni, cooked and drained
2 (6 ounce) cans tuna
1 (15 ounce) can red kidney beans,
    drained and rinsed
1 (14½ ounce) can cut green beans, drained
2 medium sized tomatoes, chopped
⅓ cup chopped onions
⅓ cup bottled Italian salad dressing
2 tablespoons lemon juice

In a large bowl, combine all ingredients. Mix well. Cover
and chill. Makes 6 to 8 servings.

TUNA ON A BED OF LETTUCE

1 (6 ounce) can tuna
3 boiled eggs, chopped
2 tablespoons onions (optional)
1 tablespoon pickle relish
2 tablespoons salad dressing
6 lettuce leaves
½ cup almond slices

In a large bowl, combine tuna, eggs, onions, relish, and
salad dressing. Mix well. Chill. Divide lettuce leaves onto 6
plates. Spoon mixture onto lettuce leaves. Top with almond
slices. Makes 6 servings.

*The people whom
the sons and daughters
find it hardest
to understand
are the fathers
and mothers,
but young people
can get along
very well with
the grandfathers
and grandmothers.*

Simeon Strunsky

SHRIMP AND ONION SALAD

12 slices party rye bread or 12 large crackers
3 tablespoons cream cheese
⅓ cup shredded cucumber
⅓ cup thinly sliced red onion
6 cups torn mixed salad greens
¾ pound shrimp, cooked,
    peeled and deveined
¼ cup bottled white wine vinaigrette
    salad dressing
1 tablespoon snipped fresh dill
Fresh dill sprigs (optional)

Spread rye bread slices or crackers with cream cheese. Top with cucumber and onion. Divide salad greens among 4 plates or bowls. Top with shrimp. In a medium bowl, combine salad dressing and dill. Mix well. Drizzle dressing over salads. Toss gently. Makes 4 servings.

*A dwarf standing
on the shoulders
of a giant
may see further
than a giant
himself.*

Robert Burton

LOBSTER PASTA SALAD

DRESSING
 cup extra virgin olive oil
½ cup cider vinegar
 garlic clove, mashed
 tablespoon sugar
 tablespoon lemon juice
salt and pepper to taste

In a medium bowl, combine all ingredients.
Mix well. Chill.

SALAD
 (16 ounce) box rotini pasta,
  cooked and drained
 cup chopped celery
 cup diced red sweet pepper
 cup diced black olives
 cup chopped scallions
 cup shredded carrots
 cup diced red onion
 cup chopped steamed lobster meat
½ cup chopped artichoke hearts
 cup canned black beans,
  rinsed and drained

In a large bowl, combine all ingredients. Mix well. Pour
dressing over salad and toss. Makes 10 to 12 servings.

*If you want
children to improve,
let them overhear
the nice things
you say about
them to others.*

Dr. Haim Ginott

SHRIMP LUNCHEON SALAD

¼ cup butter
¼ teaspoon garlic powder
8 slices bread, cubed
1 (10 ounce) package frozen peas
1 (4½ ounce) can shrimp
¼ cup salad dressing
1 teaspoon sugar
½ teaspoon salt
1 green onion, chopped
¼ cup fresh mushrooms
1 tablespoon lemon juice
6 lettuce leaves

In a large skillet, melt butter. Add butter, garlic, and bread cubes. Cook over low heat until brown. In a small saucepan, cook peas, drain and cool. Clean shrimp. In a large bowl, combine peas, shrimp, salad dressing, salt, sugar, onions, mushrooms, and lemon juice. Chill. Place lettuce leaves on plates and spoon shrimp mixture. Add browned bread crumbs. Makes 6 servings.

*It is such
a comfort to drop
the tangles of life
into God's hands
and leave
them there.*

Corrie Ten Boom

Shepherd's Table

BEEF

PORK

LAMB

POULTRY

SEAFOOD

A Happy Home

4 cups love

5 cups trust

3 cups loyalty

3 cups forgiveness

2 cups friendship

4 quarts faith

2 quarts consideration

1 barrel laughter

2 cups tenderness

2 cups kindness

2 cups hope

HUNGARIAN STEAK

2 pounds round steak, cubed
½ teaspoon onion powder
½ teaspoon garlic powder
2 tablespoons self-rising flour
½ teaspoon salt
½ teaspoon pepper
1½ teaspoons paprika
1 (10¾ ounce) can tomato soup
½ soup can water
1 cup sour cream

In a large saucepan, combine meat, onion powder, garlic powder, and flour. Mix well. Add salt, pepper, paprika, tomato soup, and water. Mix well. Cover and cook on low for 45 minutes. Combine sour cream 30 minutes before serving. Can be served over noodles or rice. Makes 6 to 8 servings.

BEEF AND GRAVY

3-4 pounds beef roast
1 envelope dry onion soup mix
½ cup beef broth
1 (10¾ ounce) can cream of mushroom soup
1 (4 ounce) can mushrooms, sliced and drained

In a slow cooker, combine all ingredients. Mix well. Cover and cook on low for 8 hours. Makes 4 to 6 servings.

It takes both rain and sunshine to make a rainbow.

EASY DOES IT ROAST

3-4 pounds beef roast
1 envelope dry onion soup mix
1 (14½ ounce) can seasoned tomatoes

In a slow cooker, place roast. Cover with onion soup mix and tomatoes. Cover and cook on low for 8 hours. Makes 4 to 6 servings.

DILLED POT ROAST

3-3½ pounds beef pot roast
1 teaspoon salt
¼ teaspoon pepper
2 teaspoons dried dill, divided
1 tablespoon vinegar
½ cup water
3 tablespoons self-rising flour
¼ cup water
¼ cup sour cream

Preheat oven to 325 degrees. Sprinkle both sides of meat with salt, pepper, and 1 teaspoon dill. In a roasting pan, place meat. In a small bowl, combine vinegar and ½ cup water. Pour over meat. Cover and cook for thirty minutes. Remove pan from oven and remove meat. In a small bowl, dissolve flour in ¼ cup water. Stir in meat drippings. Stir in additional 1 teaspoon dill and sour cream. Put meat back in pan. Place uncovered pan back in oven and cook for thirty minutes. Remove from oven, slice meat and serve with sour cream sauce over the top. Makes 6 to 8 servings.

> *I have come more and more to realize that being unwanted is the worst disease that any human being can ever experience.*
>
> Mother Teresa

OLD TIME RUMP ROAST

3 pounds rump roast
½ cup soy sauce
1 beef bouillon cube
1 bay leaf
1 teaspoon dried thyme
3 peppercorns
1 teaspoon garlic powder

Preheat oven to 325 degrees. In a roasting pan, place all ingredients. Cover and cook for 2½ hours. Makes 6 to 8 servings.

ITALIAN BEEF ROAST

3-4 pounds beef roast
1 package dry Italian dressing mix
12 ounces water

Preheat oven to 325 degrees. In a roasting pan, place roast. Sprinkle with dry Italian dressing mix. Pour water over roast. Cover and cook on low for 2½ hours. When beef is done, shred and serve with juice on crusty rolls. Makes 6 to 8 servings.

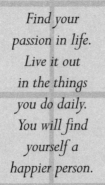

Find your passion in life. Live it out in the things you do daily. You will find yourself a happier person.

*Q*UICK AND *E*ASY *B*EEF *T*ENDERLOIN

(4 ounce) beef tenderloins, 1 inch thick, trimmed
2 teaspoon pepper
4 teaspoon salt
Cooking spray

Sprinkle steaks with salt and pepper. Coat a large skillet with cooking spray. Place skillet over medium-high heat until hot. Add tenderloins and cook over medium heat five minutes on each side or to desired degree of doneness. Makes 4 servings.

*B*ARBARIAN *S*WISS *S*TEAK

tablespoons self-rising flour
teaspoon salt
4 teaspoon pepper
½ pounds round steak, cut into
     serving-size pieces
(10¾ ounce) can cream of mushroom soup
2 soup can water
medium onion, sliced
carrot, chopped
small celery rib, chopped

Preheat oven to 350 degrees. In a large bowl combine flour, salt, and pepper. Cover steak with mixture. In a medium saucepan, warm mushroom soup and water. Mix well. In a roasting pan, place steak. In a large bowl, combine soup, onion, carrot, and celery. Pour both mixtures over steak. Cook in oven for 1½ hours. Makes 4 to 6 servings.

*Peace is not
an absence
of war;
it is a virtue,
a state of mind,
and a disposition
for benevolence,
confidence,
and justice.*

Benedict Spinoza

MARTY'S ROUND STEAK

2 pounds round steak
½ teaspoon salt
¼ teaspoon pepper
1 egg
¼ cup milk
1 cup self-rising flour
¼ cup vegetable oil

Cut steak into 4 to 6 inch wide strips. Tenderize. Salt and pepper. In a medium bowl, combine egg and milk. Mix well. In a medium bowl, place flour. Dip meat in egg mixture and then in flour. In a large skillet, add vegetable oil. Heat oil and fry steak until golden brown. Makes 4 to 6 servings.

BOAZ'S PEPPER STEAKS

2 tablespoons olive oil
2 garlic cloves, minced
4 (1 pound) 1 inch thick beef T-bone steaks
½ teaspoon salt
¼ teaspoon coarse ground black pepper

Preheat grill. In small bowl, combine oil and garlic. Mix well. Brush steaks with oil mixture. Sprinkle salt and pepper on both sides of each steak. Place steaks on grill over medium-high heat. Cook 12 to 18 minutes or until desired doneness, turning once or twice. Makes 4 servings.

It takes true humility to have true and constant gentleness.

DRENCHED SIRLOIN STEAK

1 ½ pounds sirloin steak
½ teaspoon garlic salt
½ teaspoon browning sauce
½ teaspoon salt
2 teaspoons liquid smoke flavoring
2 tablespoons canola oil
3 tablespoons Worcestershire sauce
½ tablespoon country-style Dijon mustard

Preheat grill. In medium bowl, combine garlic, sauce, salt, flavoring, oil, Worcestershire sauce, and mustard. Mix well. In a large pan, place steak. Pour half of marinade on steak. Using fork, poke several holes all over the surface of the meat. Repeat on both sides. Turn meat to coat. Allow to marinate for 15 minutes. Grill for 12 minutes or until desired doneness. Makes 2 to 4 servings.

GLAZED GRILLED STEAKS

GLAZE
½ cup pineapple preserves
½ cup teriyaki baste and glaze
2 tablespoons fresh lime juice

STEAKS
4 (1 pound) 1 inch thick steaks of choice
3 teaspoons Caribbean jerk seasoning

Heat grill. In small saucepan, combine preserves, teriyaki baste and glaze, and lime juice. Cook over low heat until preserves are melted, stirring frequently. Rub both sides of steak with jerk seasoning. Place steaks on grill over medium heat. Cook 12 to 18 minutes or until desired doneness. Turn once or twice. Brush with glaze during last 2 minutes of cooking time. Makes 4 servings.

*Have patience
with all things,
but chiefly
have patience
with yourself.*

St. Francis deSalas

FIERY FLANK STEAK

¼ cup soy sauce
¼ cup canola oil
¼ cup honey
¼ cup water
3 scallions, chopped
4 garlic cloves, finely chopped
¼ teaspoon coarse ground pepper
18 ounces lean flank steak

In large resealable plastic bag, combine soy sauce, oil, honey, water, scallions, garlic, and pepper. Shake. Add steak and seal bag, squeezing out excess air. Refrigerate at least 2 hours. Remove steak from marinade. In a small bowl, pour marinade and set aside. Grill steak and brush with marinade while cooking. Cook until desired doneness. Makes 4 to 6 servings.

THAT'S MEAT LOAF

2 pounds ground beef
1 (14½ ounce) can tomatoes
1 cup sliced bread pieces
1 small onion, chopped
1 egg
1 (10¾ ounce) can cream of mushroom soup

Preheat oven to 350 degrees. In a large bowl, combine ground beef, tomatoes, bread, onion, and egg. Mix well. Pour mixture into a 9x13 inch baking pan. Bake for 15 minutes. Remove and drain juices. In a medium bowl, combine juices and soup. Mix well. Pour over meat and return to the oven for 20 minutes. Makes 8 servings.

In order for me to do better next time, one thing is essential — to survive this time.

POOR MAN'S STEAK

1 ½ pounds ground beef, browned and crumbled
1 cup milk
¼ teaspoon pepper
1 teaspoon salt
1 small onion, finely chopped
1 cup cracker crumbs
1 teaspoon brown sugar
1 (10¾ ounce) can cream of mushroom soup
1 soup can water
Noodles or rice, cooked

In a large bowl, combine all ingredients except noodles or rice. Mix well. Pour mixture into a slow cooker or crock-pot. Cover and cook on medium for 2 to 3 hours. Serve over noodles or rice. Makes 6 to 8 servings.

WORKING WOMAN'S FAVORITE

2 pounds ground beef, browned,
    crumbled and drained
4 ribs celery, chopped
1 small green pepper, chopped
2 teaspoons sugar
½ teaspoon salt
½ teaspoon pepper
1 (10¾ ounce) can cream of mushroom soup
Warm biscuits

In a slow cooker or crock-pot, combine all ingredients except biscuits. Mix well. Cover and cook on low for 8 hours. Serve over warm biscuits. Makes 10 to 12 servings.

Friendship is either found among equals or it makes equals of those it finds. We learn to love those we have things in common with and sometimes we learn to love those we don't.

SIMPLY SALISBURY STEAK

1 (10¾ ounce) can cream of mushroom soup
1 pound ground beef
⅓ cup dry bread crumbs
1 small onion, finely chopped
1 egg, beaten
1 tablespoon vegetable oil
1½ cups sliced fresh mushrooms

In a large bowl, mix thoroughly ¼ cup soup, beef, bread crumbs, onion, and egg. Shape into 6 patties. In a large skillet over medium heat, heat vegetable oil, add patties, and brown both sides. Combine remaining soup and add mushrooms. Reduce heat to low. Cover and cook for 20 minutes. Makes 6 servings.

SKILLET ENCHILADA

1 pound ground beef, browned, crumbled
  and drained
1 (4 ounce) can green chiles, chopped
1 (10¾ ounce) can cream of mushroom soup
1 (16 ounce) can enchilada sauce
12 tortillas
1 cup shredded longhorn cheese
1 (2¼ ounce) can black olives, drained

In a large skillet, combine beef, chiles, soup, and sauce. Simmer for 20 minutes. Roll tortillas and slide them under sauce in the skillet. Sprinkle cheese over top. Let stand until cheese melts. Sprinkle with olives. Makes 12 servings.

If you are exchanging greetings only with your own circle, are you doing anything exceptional?

CORNELIUS' CHOPS

tablespoons vegetable oil
alt and pepper to taste
pork chops
medium onion, sliced
(10¾ ounce) can cream of chicken soup
¼ cup ketchup
teaspoons Worcestershire sauce

n a large saucepan, heat vegetable oil. Salt and pepper
ork chops and brown in oil. Top with onion slices. In a
mall bowl, blend soup, ketchup, and Worcestershire
auce. Pour mixture over chops. Simmer 45 to 60 minutes.
Makes 6 servings.

SAVORY ONION CHOPS

(¾ inch) pork chops
package onion soup mix

Preheat oven to 350 degrees. Roll pork chops in onion soup
mix. Wrap in foil and seal. On a baking sheet, place pork
chops. Cook for 1 hour and 15 minutes. Makes 4 servings.

CREOLE PORK CHOPS

⅛ cup water
(1.2 ounce) package Creole seasoning
(¾ inch) pork chops

Preheat oven 350 degrees. In a roasting pan, place water.
Season pork chops with Creole seasoning. Cover. Cook for
0 to 75 minutes. Makes 4 servings.

Create a good person in your children; let them know they are unique and wonderful. They can only make a difference if they feel good about who they are.

JUST PEACHY CHOPS

¼ cup vegetable oil
4 pork chops
¼ cup sliced onions
¼ cup packed light brown sugar
1 teaspoon ginger
½ teaspoon salt
1 teaspoon soy sauce
¼ cup cider vinegar
½ cup water
2 cups frozen peaches
1 teaspoon cornstarch
2 tablespoons water

*Use obstacles
as springboards
to the next place
you need to be,
don't let them
get you down.
Get on top
of them.*

In a large skillet, heat vegetable oil and brown chops. Remove chops from skillet and pour off fat. Return chops to skillet. Add onions. In a medium bowl, combine sugar, ginger, and salt. Mix well. Pour mixture over chops. In a medium bowl, combine soy sauce, vinegar, and water. Mix well. Pour over chops. Cover and reduce heat and simmer for 45 to 50 minutes. Add peaches and simmer, covered, for 10 minutes. In a small bowl, combine cornstarch with 2 tablespoons water. Mix until lumps are gone. Stir liquid into skillet to thicken. Serve gravy over meat and peaches. Makes 4 servings.

COURTYARD RIBS

1 teaspoon salt
½ teaspoon pepper
5 pounds pork ribs
3 cups favorite barbecue sauce

Preheat oven to 350 degrees. Salt and pepper ribs. In a 9x1 inch baking pan, place ribs. Pour barbecue sauce over ribs. Cover with foil. Cook for 2 hours. Makes 2 to 4 servings.

SWEET PORK

1 (16 ounce) can pineapple tidbits
2 tablespoons soy sauce
1½ tablespoons cider vinegar
2 teaspoons cornstarch
2 teaspoons sesame oil
1½ pounds boneless pork, cut into 1 inch chunks

Drain pineapple, reserving ½ cup juice. Set pineapple aside. In a small bowl, combine reserved juice, soy sauce, vinegar, and cornstarch. Stir until cornstarch is dissolved. Set aside. In a wok or large skillet, heat oil over high heat. Add pork and cook until well browned. Stir in reserved pineapple. Add reserved juice mixture. Bring to a boil. Reduce heat to low. Simmer, stirring occasionally, until pork is cooked, 5 to 15 minutes. Makes 2 to 4 servings.

PORK AND VEGETABLES

Salt and pepper to taste
4 boneless pork chops, sliced
2 tablespoons butter
1½ cup sliced fresh mushrooms
½ teaspoon dried, crushed rosemary leaves
1 (10¾ ounce) can cream of mushroom soup
½ pound fresh green beans, cut into 2 inch pieces
2 tablespoons water

Salt and pepper chops. In a large skillet over medium heat, melt butter and brown chops. Stir in mushrooms, rosemary, and soup. Mix well. Cover and cook for 10 minutes. Add green beans and water. Stir and cook for 3 to 5 minutes, until desired crispness of green beans is achieved. Makes 4 servings.

*Choose each word
with care
and say only
what you mean.*

DREAMY PORK CHOPS

1 ounce cooking oil
Salt and pepper to taste
4 pork chops, trimmed
½ pound mushrooms, sliced
1 (10¾ ounce) can cream of mushroom soup
1 cup milk

In a large skillet, add cooking oil. Salt and pepper chops
and brown on both sides. Remove chops from skillet.
Add mushrooms to skillet and cook. Stir until lightly
browned and liquid has evaporated. Stir in soup and milk.
Add chops to sauce. Cook, covered, over low heat for
about 30 minutes, or until meat is tender. Makes 4 servings.

*Children see
and hear
what you do,
more than hear
what you say.*

CHOPS IN A POT

½ teaspoon salt
⅛ teaspoon pepper
½ cup chopped onions
4 pork chops
1 (10¾ ounce) can cream of mushroom soup

Salt and pepper chops. In a slow cooker or crock-pot, place
onions, chops, and soup. Cover and cook on low for 6 to 8
hours. Makes 4 servings.

TOMATO AND BASIL CHOPS

4 pork chops
½ teaspoon salt
1 (26 ounce) jar tomato and basil sauce

Preheat oven to 350 degrees. In a 9x13 inch baking pan,
place chops. Salt and pour sauce over chops. Cover and
bake for 20 minutes. Uncover and bake for 10 minutes.
Makes 4 servings.

ITALIAN PORK

-4 pounds pork roast
 package dry Italian dressing mix
2 ounces water

reheat oven to 325 degrees. In a roasting pan, place roast.
prinkle with dressing mix. Pour water over roast. Cover
nd cook for 2½ hours. When pork is done, shred and serve
vith juice on crusty rolls. Makes 4 to 6 servings.

CENTER-CUT PORK ROAST

 pounds center-cut, boneless or
 rib-end pork loin roast
 tablespoons oil, preferably olive
 tablespoons molasses
 ½ teaspoons dry garam masala seasoning
 teaspoon salt
/2 teaspoon coarse-ground pepper
/2 teaspoon garlic powder
/4 teaspoon anise seeds

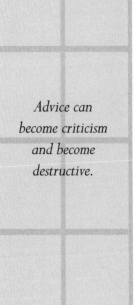

*Advice can
become criticism
and become
destructive.*

reheat oven to 450 degrees. In a roasting pan, place roast.
n small bowl, combine oil, molasses, garam masala, salt,
epper, garlic powder, and anise seeds. Rub mixture over
oast. Cook for 15 minutes. Reduce oven temperature
o 350 degrees. Roast for about 1½ hours. Let stand 15
ninutes before slicing. Makes 4 to 6 servings.

PORK ROAST WITH CHERRIES

2 pounds boneless pork roast
1 (21 ounce) can cherry pie filling
½ cup raisins
2 tablespoons lemon juice
½ teaspoon cinnamon

Preheat oven to 325 degrees. In a roasting pan, cook roast uncovered for 1 hour. In a medium bowl, combine pie filling, raisins, lemon juice, and cinnamon. Mix well. Spoon mixture over roast. Return to oven and cook 30 minutes. Let stand for 10 minutes before slicing. Makes 4 to 6 servings.

CHERRY AND ALMOND GLAZED PORK ROAST

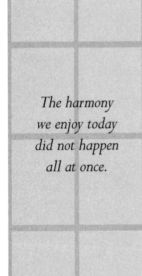

The harmony we enjoy today did not happen all at once.

2 pounds rolled pork loin roast
½ teaspoon salt
¼ teaspoon pepper
1 (12 ounce) jar cherry preserves
2 tablespoons light corn syrup
¼ cup red wine vinegar
¼ teaspoon salt
¼ teaspoon cinnamon
¼ teaspoon nutmeg
¼ teaspoon cloves
¼ cup slivered toasted almonds

Preheat oven to 325 degrees. Rub roast with salt and pepper. In a shallow roasting pan with rack, place roast, fat side up. Cook uncovered for 2 to 2½ hours. In a medium saucepan, combine preserves, syrup, vinegar, salt, cinnamon, nutmeg, and cloves. Heat to boiling and simmer for 2 minutes, stirring often. Keep sauce warm. Add toasted almonds. When roast has baked 2 to 2½ hours, spoon enough sauce over it to glaze. Return to oven for 30 more minutes, basting often. Pour remaining sauce over roast. Makes 4 to 6 servings.

MUSTARD AND ONION PORK CUTLETS

cup whole milk
tablespoon Dijon mustard
tablespoon chopped onions
⅓ cups stuffing mix
(3 ounce) pork cutlets
cooking spray

Preheat oven to 425 degrees. In a large bowl, combine milk, mustard, onion, and stuffing mix. Beat pork cutlets with a meat tenderizer. Coat the pork with the stuffing mixture, and place in milk mixture. Refrigerate for 30 minutes. Coat a 9x13 inch baking pan with cooking spray. Place pork in baking pan, and discard milk mixture. Bake for 20 minutes. Makes 4 servings.

MARINATED PORK TENDERLOIN

½ cup soy sauce
¼ cup sugar
½ teaspoon garlic powder
tablespoons ketchup
2-3 pounds pork tenderloin
cooking spray

In a large bowl, combine soy sauce, sugar, garlic powder, and ketchup. Mix well. Add pork, cover and refrigerate overnight. Coat a 9x13 inch baking pan, with cooking spray, place pork and marinade. Bake at 350 degrees uncovered for 1½ hours. Makes 4 to 6 servings.

The road to success is always under construction.

John W. Patten

GENESIS 6:10 STEAK

1 (3 inch) sliced ham, uncooked
Cooking spray
¼ cup packed brown sugar
1 tablespoon cornstarch
⅛ teaspoon ginger
1 (8½ ounce) can crushed pineapple, undrained
1 tablespoon lemon juice

Preheat oven to 325 degrees. Slash edge of ham in several places. Coat a shallow dish with cooking spray and place ham. In a medium saucepan, combine sugar, cornstarch, ginger, pineapple, and lemon juice. Heat to boiling, stirring constantly. Pour over ham. Cover with foil and bake for 45 minutes. Makes 1 serving.

COMPANY HAM

3-4 pounds ham, cooked
8 cloves
8 ounces pineapple juice
1 cup packed brown sugar
2 tablespoons molasses
½ teaspoon dry mustard
4 cherries

Preheat oven to 350 degrees. In a roasting pan, place ham. Score ham slightly. Place cloves in scores. In a medium bowl, mix pineapple juice, sugar, molasses, and mustard. Pour ingredients over ham. Place cherries on top. Cover with foil and bake for 40 minutes or until warm throughout. Slice and serve. Makes 16 servings.

God loves you where you are, but God also loves you too much to leave you there.

GRILLED LAMB CHOPS

3 tablespoons sherry vinegar
2 teaspoons chopped fresh mint leaves
1 tablespoon packed brown sugar
3 tablespoons cooking oil
salt and pepper to taste
8 lamb chops

In a small saucepan, mix together vinegar, mint, and brown sugar. Heat until simmering, set aside. Add oil to mixture. Salt and pepper chops. Coat with mixture. Grill chops while basting both sides with the mint marinade. Cook until desired doneness. Makes 8 servings.

SMOKED LEG OF LAMB

5-6 pounds leg of lamb
1/2 cup lemon juice
2 tablespoons garlic powder
1 tablespoon black pepper
4 strips bacon
1 medium green pepper, sliced
1 lemon, sliced

Rub lamb with lemon juice, garlic powder, and black pepper. Place bacon, green pepper, and lemon slices on lamb. In a smoker, place leg directly on rack and smoke approximately 4 hours.

SAUCE
6 tablespoons melted butter
3 lemons, juiced
2 tablespoons Worcestershire sauce
1 tablespoon water

In a medium saucepan, combine all ingredients. Heat. Serve with lamb as a garnish. Makes 6 to 8 servings.

*Experience
is not
what happens
to a man,
it is what a man does
with
what happens
to him.*

Aldous Huxley

95

SMOTHERED LAMB AND ORANGES

1 carrot, cut into ½ inch slices
1 onion, sliced thinly
1 cup red cooking wine
1 cup water
1 laurel leaf
2 cloves, minced
1 tablespoon self-rising flour
4 lamb chops, cut each into three pieces
Salt and pepper to taste
Paprika to taste
1 teaspoon butter
3 oranges, peeled and cut into slices

In a large bowl, mix carrot, onion, wine, water, laurel, cloves, and flour. Mix well. Marinate lamb overnight in mixture. Remove lamb from marinade and season with salt, pepper, and paprika. In a large skillet, melt butter. Fry lamb in butter, add marinade. Cover and simmer for about 30 minutes. Place orange slices on top. Makes 4 servings.

A kind word
can grow
a garden
in someone's
heart.

SAUCED LAMB

5-6 pounds leg of lamb
Salt and pepper to taste
1 cup water
1 (8 ounce) jar mint jelly
2 tablespoons flour

Preheat oven to 325 degrees. Rub lamb with salt and pepper. In a roasting pan, pour water. Place lamb in water. Cover loosely with aluminum foil. Cook for 2 hours. Remove lamb from oven. In a medium saucepan, pour juices from lamb. Cook over medium heat. Add jelly and flour. Mix well until all lumps are gone and jelly is melted. Pour mixture over lamb and serve. Makes 8 to 10 servings.

UNFRIED CHICKEN

2 cups self-rising flour
1 cup packaged bread crumbs
Salt and pepper to taste
4 chicken breasts, boneless, skinless
1 cup skim milk
Cooking spray

Preheat oven to 400 degrees. In a medium bowl, mix flour, bread crumbs, salt, and pepper (to taste) together. In a large bowl, pour milk and dip chicken in milk. Roll in flour mixture until breast is well-coated. Coat a 9x13 inch baking pan with cooking spray. Place chicken in the baking pan and cook for 50 minutes. Makes 4 servings.

CASHEW CHICKEN

1 pound chicken fillet
3 tablespoons oil
1 clove garlic, chopped
1 teaspoon soy sauce
½ cup whole cashews

Chop chicken into bite-size pieces. In a large skillet, heat oil. Cook chicken and garlic for 5 minutes. Add soy sauce and cashews. Cook for 3 minutes. Makes 4 to 6 servings.

Your grandmother always thinks what you do is just wonderful. Even the slamming noise of the front door will be missed in years to come. Treasure the moments.

CHICKEN GARDEN SAUTÉ

4 boneless, skinless chicken breasts halves
1 tablespoon olive oil
½ teaspoon crushed rosemary
Salt and pepper to taste
12 small black, ripe, pitted olives
1 (14½ ounce) can diced tomatoes
1 green pepper, cut in thin strips
1 large carrot, cut in 3 inch julienne strips

In a large skillet, brown chicken in oil. Sprinkle with rosemary, salt, and pepper. Combine olives, tomatoes, green pepper, and carrots. Bring to boil. Cover and cook 5 minutes over medium heat. Uncover, cook over medium-high heat for 5 minutes or until thickened. Makes 4 servings.

Memories remain in the heart. Make happy ones today.

CHICKEN PARMESAN

Cooking spray
2 eggs
1 cup bread crumbs
¼ cup fresh shredded Parmesan cheese
½ teaspoon onion powder
½ teaspoon garlic powder
½ teaspoon oregano
1 pound chicken breasts, boneless, skinless
1½ cups pasta sauce
4 ounces mozzarella cheese, sliced

Preheat oven to 425 degrees. Coat a 9x13 inch baking pan with cooking spray. In a medium bowl, place eggs and beat. In a large bowl, combine bread crumbs, Parmesan cheese, onion powder, garlic powder, and oregano. Mix well. Dip each chicken breast into eggs, then roll in bread crumbs to coat on all sides. Place chicken breasts in baking pan and bake 30 to 35 minutes, until golden brown and cooked thoroughly. Pour pasta sauce over chicken. Top with mozzarella cheese slices. Reduce oven temperature to 375 degrees. Cook until sauce is hot and cheese is melted, about 5 to 10 minutes. Makes 4 servings.

ROSEMARY CHICKEN

Cooking spray
1½ tablespoons minced garlic
2¼ tablespoons chopped fresh rosemary leaves
1½ teaspoons oregano
¾ teaspoon onion powder
½ teaspoon pepper
¼ cup chicken broth
1½ pounds chicken breasts, boneless, skinless

Prepare a hot grill and coat with cooking spray. In a small bowl, combine garlic, rosemary, oregano, onion powder, pepper, and chicken broth. Mix well. In a baking pan, place chicken and pour broth mixture over chicken. Turn several times to coat on all sides. Grill chicken breasts for 10-12 minutes per side, until browned and cooked thoroughly. Makes 4 to 6 servings.

GRILLED CHICKEN SOUTHWESTERN STYLE

1 tablespoon chicken broth
1 tablespoon lime juice
½ teaspoon chili powder
¼ teaspoon pepper
1 teaspoon minced garlic
1½ pounds chicken breasts, boneless, skinless
Cooking spray
1½ cups chunky-style salsa

In a medium bowl, combine chicken broth, lime juice, chili powder, pepper, and garlic. Mix well. In a shallow baking pan, place chicken. Pour marinade over chicken. Cover, marinade and chill overnight. Prepare a medium hot grill and lightly coat with cooking spray. Remove chicken from marinade and grill 8 to 10 minutes per side, until cooked thoroughly. Place chicken on plate and top with salsa. Makes 4 to 6 servings.

*Introverts
are not
party poopers,
they just
get pooped
at parties*

THE BISHOP'S CHICKEN

1 pound chicken breasts, boneless, skinless
1 teaspoon onion powder
1 teaspoon minced garlic
1 cup Italian salad dressing
¼ cup water
Cooking spray

In a 9x13 inch baking pan, place chicken breasts. Season both sides with onion powder. In a small bowl, combine Italian salad dressing, water, and garlic. Mix well. Pour mixture over chicken. Cover with plastic wrap and marinate in refrigerator at least 2 hours or overnight. Prepare a hot grill and coat with cooking spray. Remove chicken breasts from marinade. Grill 8 to 10 minutes per side, until cooked thoroughly. Makes 4 servings.

LEMON GRILLED CHICKEN

3 tablespoons olive oil
3 tablespoons fresh lemon juice
1 tablespoon honey
1 tablespoon chopped fresh rosemary
¼ teaspoon salt
2 garlic cloves, minced
3 pounds frying chicken, cut up and skin
   removed if desired

In a small bowl, combine olive oil, lemon juice, honey, rosemary, salt, and cloves. Mix well. In a large shallow baking pan, place chicken. Brush or rub oil mixture on chicken pieces, using all of mixture. Cover and chill at least 1 hour. Heat grill. When ready to grill, remove chicken from marinade, reserving marinade. Place chicken on gas grill over medium heat or on charcoal grill 4 to 6 inches from medium coals. Brushing with marinade, cook 8 to 10 minutes until cooked thoroughly. Makes 4 to 6 servings.

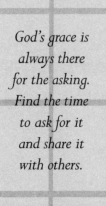

God's grace is always there for the asking. Find the time to ask for it and share it with others.

Heavenly Chicken Wings

teaspoons canola oil
small onion, minced
clove garlic, minced
teaspoons peeled and shredded fresh ginger
¼ teaspoon salt
⅛ teaspoon crushed red pepper flakes
tablespoons vinegar, preferably apple cider
⅓ cup ketchup
½ cup apricot preserves
½ pounds chicken wings
Cooking spray

Preheat oven to 350 degrees. In a medium saucepan, heat oil. Add onion, garlic, ginger, salt, and pepper flakes. Cook, stirring occasionally, until softened, 3 minutes. Add vinegar, cook 1 minute. Stir in ketchup and preserves, bring to boil. Reduce heat to low, simmer until mixture is thickened and reduced to about 1 cup, about 20 minutes. Coat grill with cooking spray. Reserve ¼ cup sauce. Cut wings at joints and discard tips. In a large bowl, toss chicken pieces with remaining sauce. Place chicken pieces on grill and cook while brushing occasionally with reserved sauce. Remove chicken when cooked thoroughly. Makes 6 to 8 servings.

With everyone pulling on you, find a way to take a day to rest and learn more about yourself.

LEAN TURKEY BURGERS

1 pound ground turkey
⅓ cup cracker crumbs
1½ teaspoons onion powder
2 tablespoons ketchup
1 tablespoon teriyaki sauce
Pepper to taste

In a medium bowl, combine all ingredients. Mix well. Form mixture into patties. Chill before cooking. Preheat broiler on high heat and cook burgers 4 inches from heat until cooked thoroughly, about 5 minutes per side. Makes 4 to 6 servings.

SURPRISE MEAT LOAF

Cooking spray
¾ pound ground turkey
¾ cup cornflake crumbs
¼ cup chopped onion
½ cup tomato sauce
1½ teaspoons Worcestershire sauce
1 large egg
Pepper to taste

Preheat oven to 350 degrees. Lightly coat 8x4 inch loaf pan with cooking spray. In a large bowl, combine all ingredients. Mix well. Place meat mixture into loaf pan. Bake for 40 minutes, until firm to the touch. Makes 4 to 6 servings.

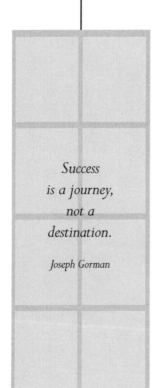

*Success
is a journey,
not a
destination.*

Joseph Gorman

HOT ITALIAN TURKEY SANDWICH

2 tablespoons butter
2 small carrots, thinly sliced diagonally
1 medium onion, chopped
¼ cup celery
¾ teaspoon snipped fresh thyme leaves
1 (10½ ounce) can turkey gravy
½ pound turkey, sliced
4 slices Italian bread

In 2-quart saucepan over medium heat, melt butter. Cook carrots, onions, celery, and thyme until vegetables are tender, stirring occasionally. Stir in gravy. Heat to boiling. Add turkey. Heat thoroughly, stirring occasionally. Divide turkey and gravy mixture evenly over the four slices of bread. Makes 4 servings.

TURKEY CHEESEBURGERS

Cooking spray
1½ pounds ground turkey
1 teaspoon Worcestershire sauce
1 teaspoon onion powder
4 small portabello mushrooms
4 slices Swiss cheese
1 tablespoon deli-style mustard
4 sandwich rolls

Prepare a medium-hot grill and lightly coat with cooking spray. In a large bowl, combine turkey, Worcestershire sauce, and onion powder. Mix well. Shape mixture into 4 patties. When ready to grill, place burgers on grill and cook 6 to 7 minutes, per side, over a medium-hot grill. Lightly coat square foil sheet with cooking spray. Place mushrooms on sheet and grill next to the burgers until tender. When burgers are cooked thoroughly, top each with one slice of cheese. Cook until cheese is melted. Spread mustard on bottom half of each bun, top with burger, mushrooms, and other favorite ingredients. Makes 6 servings.

Human beings are the language of God.

CURRY TURKEY BURGERS

1 pound ground turkey
1 teaspoon onion powder
¼ teaspoon garlic powder
¼ cup bread crumbs
3 teaspoons curry powder

In a large bowl, combine all ingredients. Mix well. Shape mixture into patties. Grill patties on hot grill until cooked thoroughly. Makes 4 servings.

TURKEY VALLEY VEGGIE BURGERS

Cooking spray
1½ pounds ground turkey
1 small zucchini, shredded
1 tablespoon onion flakes
1 large carrot, peeled and shredded
1 tablespoon Worcestershire sauce
1 tablespoon mustard
1 tablespoon ketchup
Salt and pepper to taste

Prepare a hot grill and lightly coat with cooking spray. In a large bowl, combine all ingredients. Mix well. Shape into patties. Grill patties on hot grill until cooked thoroughly. Makes 4 to 6 servings.

The gift without the giver is bare; who gives himself with his alms, feeds three, himself, his hungry neighbor, and me.

James Russell Lowell

SPICY TURKEY KABOBS

½ cup mayonnaise
1¼ teaspoons hot pepper sauce
1½ pounds turkey tenders, cut in chunks
1 medium red bell pepper, cut in chunks
1 medium yellow pepper, cut in chunks
2 medium onions, cut in quarters

In a medium bowl, combine mayonnaise and hot pepper sauce. Blend well. Stir in turkey. Marinate in sauce, at room temperature, 15 to 20 minutes. On metal skewers, alternately thread turkey, peppers, and onions. Grill until turkey is cooked thoroughly and vegetables are tender. Turn frequently. Baste turkey and vegetables with mayonnaise mixture several times while cooking. Makes 4 to 6 servings.

*Grandparents
are people
who come
to your house,
spoil the
children,
and then
go home.*

Anonymous

BAKED CATFISH

¾ cup ketchup
¼ cup butter or margarine
1 tablespoon balsamic vinegar
1 tablespoon Worcestershire sauce
1 teaspoon Dijon mustard
½ teaspoon Jamaican jerk seasoning
1 garlic clove, minced
10 (3 to 4 ounce) catfish fillets
⅛ teaspoon pepper
Cooking spray
Fresh parsley

Preheat oven to 400 degrees. In a small saucepan, stir together ketchup, butter, vinegar, Worcestershire sauce, mustard, seasoning, and garlic. Cook over medium-low heat for 10 minutes, stirring occasionally. Sprinkle catfish with pepper. Coat aluminum foil-lined broiler with cooking spray, arrange fish in an even layer. Pour sauce over catfish. Bake catfish for 10 to 12 minutes or until fish flakes with a fork. Garnish with parsley. Makes 10 servings.

PETER'S FAVORITE COD

Cooking spray
1½ pounds cod fillets
1½ cups sour cream
1 teaspoon horseradish
2 teaspoons mustard
1 cup shredded Parmesan cheese

Preheat oven to 350 degrees. Lightly coat a 9x13 inch baking pan with cooking spray, place fish fillets. In a small bowl, combine sour cream, horseradish, and mustard, and mix until smooth. Spread mixture over top of fish fillets and sprinkle with Parmesan cheese. Bake 20 to 25 minutes, or until fish flakes easily in thickest portion. Makes 4 to 6 servings.

There are three kinds of people in the world, those that make it happen, those that watch it happen and those that throw up their hands and say, "what happened?"

Anonymous

ANDREW'S FISH FILLETS

Cooking spray
2 pounds of your favorite fish fillets
4 large onions, sliced
1/2 cup mayonnaise
1/2 teaspoon garlic powder
1/4 cup shredded Parmesan cheese
2 tablespoons Worcestershire sauce
2 tablespoons lemon juice

Preheat oven to 350 degrees. Lightly coat 9x13 inch baking pan with cooking spray. Cut fish into individual portions. Arrange onions on bottom of baking pan and place fish pieces on top. In a small bowl, combine mayonnaise, garlic powder, cheese, Worcestershire sauce, and lemon juice. Mix until blended. Spread mixture over fish pieces and bake in preheated oven 35 to 40 minutes, or until fish flakes easily. Makes 4 to 6 servings.

MARINATED SALMON STEAKS

1/2 cup packed dark brown sugar
2 tablespoons soy sauce
2 tablespoons lemon juice
4 tablespoons melted butter
4 salmon steaks

In a large bowl, combine sugar, soy sauce, lemon juice, and butter. Marinate steaks for 15 minutes. Place on hot grill for 8 to 10 minutes. Turn only once. Makes 4 servings.

*There is
no free lunch;
you have to
pay the piper.*

MOMMA'S FRIED SALMON PATTIES

1 (14¾ ounce) can pink salmon
1 egg
2 tablespoons self-rising flour
¼ cup vegetable oil

In a large bowl, combine salmon, egg, and flour. In a large skillet, heat oil. Shape salmon by hand into patties. Fry until golden brown. Makes 2 to 4 servings.

BREADED SNAPPER

1 teaspoon salt
2 cups corn meal
2 eggs, beaten
½ cup milk
1½ pounds fresh snapper
½ cup oil

In a large bowl, combine salt and corn meal. In a medium bowl, combine eggs and milk. Mix well. Dip each piece of fish in egg mixture. Coat with corn meal. In a large skillet, heat oil. Fry each piece of fish until golden brown. Makes 2 to 4 servings.

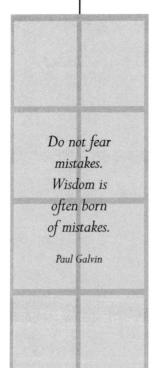

Do not fear mistakes. Wisdom is often born of mistakes.

Paul Galvin

LEMONY FISH

Cooking spray
1½ pounds any white fish
4 teaspoons olive oil
½ teaspoon salt
⅓ teaspoon lemon pepper
1 tablespoon dried parsley
2 tablespoons lemon juice

Preheat oven to 375 degrees. Lightly coat a 9x13 inch
baking pan and arrange fillets. Drizzle with oil and season
with salt and lemon pepper. Sprinkle with parsley and
lemon juice. Bake for 10 minutes or until fish is opaque
throughout. Makes 6 to 8 servings.

TOMATO PEPPER FLOUNDER

Cooking spray
1½ pounds flounder
4 cups bread crumbs
1 teaspoon onion powder
½ teaspoon garlic powder
¼ teaspoon pepper
1 tablespoon lemon juice
1½ tablespoons melted margarine
¼ cup shredded Parmesan cheese, divided
1 cup chopped tomatoes

Preheat oven to 400 degrees. Lightly spray 9x13 inch
baking pan and arrange fish in a single layer. In a medium
bowl, combine bread crumbs, onion powder, garlic powder,
pepper, lemon juice, margarine, and ¼ cup cheese. Blend
well. Spread bread mixture over fish and top with tomatoes.
Sprinkle remaining cheese on top and bake for 15 minutes,
until fish flakes easily when tested in thickest part. Makes 4
to 6 servings.

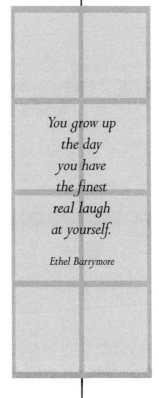

*You grow up
the day
you have
the finest
real laugh
at yourself.*

Ethel Barrymore

IN THE BAG SHRIMP TERIYAKI

2 tablespoons teriyaki sauce
1½ tablespoons lime juice
1 tablespoon packed brown sugar
½ teaspoon ginger
2 garlic cloves, minced
1½ pounds shrimp, peeled and cleaned

In a large zip-lock bag, combine teriyaki sauce, lime juice, sugar, ginger, and garlic. Add shrimp and seal bag, turning to evenly coat shrimp. Marinate and chill overnight. Grill for 3 to 5 minutes. Makes 6 to 8 servings.

GRILLIN' SHRIMP

1 cup lemon juice
1 pound large tiger shrimp, peeled and cleaned

In a small bowl, place lemon juice. Dip each shrimp into lemon juice and place on grill. Grill for 3 to 5 minutes. Makes 4 to 6 servings.

*Don't lie;
always tell
the truth to
your neighbor.
Trust can never
be built back
after you tell
someone
something that
is not true.*

SHRIMP SCAMPI

stick butter
cloves garlic, pressed
¼ cup lemon juice
pounds raw shrimp, peeled
salt to taste

n a medium saucepan, melt butter and sauté garlic, then
add lemon juice. In a shallow baking pan, arrange shrimp
n a single layer. Pour garlic butter over shrimp and salt
ightly. Broil 2 minutes. Turn shrimp and broil 2 more
minutes. Reserve garlic butter and serve separately.
Makes 10 to 12 servings.

SCALLOP AND VEGGIE STIR-FRY

Cooking spray
¼ cup water
cups sliced carrots
cups cherry tomatoes
cups broccoli florets
cups cauliflower florets
medium baking potatoes, cooked and cubed
cups whole mushrooms
cups shredded cabbage
ounces scallops
cup teriyaki sauce
ounces canned water chestnuts, sliced

n a large skillet or wok, coat with cooking spray. Add ¼ cup
water. Over medium-high heat, combine all ingredients but
teriyaki sauce, stirring frequently, until vegetables are tender
and scallops are cooked thoroughly. Pour in teriyaki sauce and
cook until heated thoroughly. Makes 4 to 6 servings.

*The best thing about
the future
is that it comes
only one day
at a time.*

Abraham Lincoln

NUT-CRUSTED HALIBUT

¾ cup chopped walnuts or macadamia nuts
¼ cup seasoned bread crumbs
1 egg
4 (6 ounce) halibut fillets ½"- ¾" thick
4 tablespoons butter

In a medium bowl, mix nut and bread crumbs. In a small bowl, beat egg. Dip fillets in egg and then in nut mixture. In a large frying pan, melt butter and sauté fillets for 5 minutes on each side. Makes 4 servings.

BAKED SEA BASS WITH SPINACH

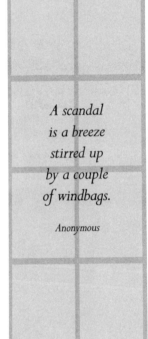

A scandal is a breeze stirred up by a couple of windbags.

Anonymous

¼ cup orange juice
2 pounds sea bass, cut into 6 fillets
1½ pounds baby spinach, washed
1 (10 ounce) package mushrooms, sliced
2 tablespoons olive oil

Preheat oven to 450 degrees. In a large bowl, combine orange juice and bass. Marinate for 15 minutes. In another large bowl, toss together spinach, sliced mushrooms, and oil. Coat a 9x13 inch baking pan with cooking spray. Pour spinach mixture into dish and place fish fillets on top. Cover dish and bake for 10 minutes. Uncover and bake for 5 minutes or until fish is flaky and opaque. Makes 6 servings.

The
Good Earth

VEGETABLES

PASTA

RICE

CASSEROLES

Life's Recipes

1 cup good thoughts

1 cup kind deeds

1 cup consideration for others

2 cups sacrifice for others

3 cups forgiveness

2 cups faults, well beaten

4 cups prayer and faith

8 cups blessings

Sprinkle of tears

for each — joy, sorrow, and

sympathy for others

MARTHA'S POTATOES

Cooking spray
2 large baking potatoes, unpeeled, sliced
   crosswise very thin
4 tablespoons fat-free Italian dressing

Preheat oven to 500 degrees. Lightly coat baking sheet
with cooking spray. In a medium size bowl, place sliced
potatoes. Add fat-free Italian dressing and toss until
potatoes are evenly coated. Arrange potato slices on a
baking sheet. Bake for 20 minutes or until lightly brown
on both sides. Turn when necessary. Makes 2 servings.

FLUFFY WHITE POTATOES

4 quarts water
4 large potatoes, cleaned, peeled and sliced
Salt and pepper to taste
¼ cup whole milk
1 cup light sour cream
2 tablespoons butter

In a large saucepan, bring water to a boil. Add potatoes.
Salt and pepper. Cook until soft. Drain water. Blend with
an electric mixer. Add milk, sour cream, and butter. Whip
until fluffy. Makes 4 to 6 servings.

*Better is
a dish of
vegetables
where love is,
than a huge
meal where
hatred
abounds.*

GREEN BEAN DISH

1 (28 ounce) can green beans
1 (8 ounce) can chicken broth
1 small onion, chopped

Empty green beans into a strainer and rinse thoroughly. In a medium saucepan, place green beans. Add chicken broth and onion. Cook on medium heat for 10 minutes. Makes 4 to 6 servings.

ALMOND GREEN BEANS

⅓ cup slivered almonds
½ stick margarine
¼ teaspoon garlic salt
3 tablespoons lemon juice
2 (16 ounce) cans French-style green beans

In a medium saucepan, cook almonds in margarine, garlic salt, and lemon juice until slightly golden brown. Add drained green beans to mixture and heat. Makes 4 to 6 servings.

GARLIC GREEN BEANS

3 tablespoons olive oil
4 garlic cloves, minced
2 pounds fresh green beans, trimmed
½ cup chicken broth
1 teaspoon sugar
½ teaspoon salt
¼ teaspoon pepper

In a large skillet over medium heat, place oil. Add garlic and beans, tossing to coat. Add broth, sugar, salt, and pepper. Simmer for 10 minutes or until green beans are crisp tender. Makes 4 to 6 servings.

> Great achievement is usually born of great sacrifice, and is never the result of selfishness.
>
> *Napoleon Hill*

COPPER CARROTS

2 pounds cooked carrots, peeled and sliced
1 (10¾ ounce) can tomato soup
1 cup sugar
½ cup vinegar
1 tablespoon Worcestershire sauce
Salt and pepper to taste
1 small onion, chopped
1 bell pepper, chopped

In a large bowl, combine all ingredients. Mix well. Chill and marinate overnight. Serve cold. Makes 4 to 6 servings.

SUGAR CARROTS

2 tablespoons packed brown sugar
½ cup orange juice
4 cups sliced carrots

Preheat oven to 350 degrees. In a medium bowl, combine sugar and orange juice. In a 1-quart baking dish, place carrots and add mixture. Bake for 40 minutes. Makes 2 to 4 servings.

MARY'S VEGETABLES

1 cup fresh or frozen mixed vegetables
1 cup water
2 bouillon cubes

In a medium saucepan, combine all ingredients. Mix well. Bring to a boil. Reduce heat. Cover and simmer until vegetables are tender. Do not overcook. Makes 1 serving.

Having many people to love is the advantage of being old.

MEDLEY IN MICROWAVE

2 cups fresh broccoli flowerets
2 cups fresh cauliflowerets
2 large carrots, scraped and cut on diagonal
   in ¼ inch slices
1 teaspoon butter, cut into small pieces
¼ teaspoon dried basil leaves
¼ teaspoon dried dill weed
Salt and pepper to taste

In a 1¼-quart baking dish, place vegetables. Sprinkle with butter and seasonings. Mix well. Place glass cover on dish. Cook in microwave on high power for 3 minutes. Remove and stir. Return to microwave for 3 minutes, or until vegetables are done. Salt and pepper. Makes 4 servings.

FRIED CORN IN CREAM

1 stick butter
2 (16 ounce) packages frozen whole kernel corn
1 cup whipping cream
1 tablespoon chopped green onion
1 tablespoon sugar
1 teaspoon salt

In a large skillet, melt butter and add corn. Mix well. Add whipping cream, green onion, sugar, and salt. Cook on medium heat. Stirring constantly, heat until most of the whipping cream and butter is absorbed into the corn. Makes 5 to 8 servings.

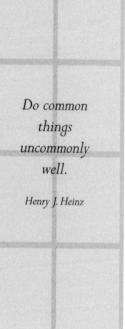

*Do common
things
uncommonly
well.*

Henry J. Heinz

CORNFIELD CREAM CHEESE CORN

1 (2 pound) bag frozen whole kernel corn
¼ cup water
1 (8 ounce) package cream cheese
Salt and pepper to taste

In a medium pot, cook corn in water until tender. Drain off all excess water. Add cream cheese. Mix well and stir gently until cheese is melted. Add salt and pepper. Makes 4 to 6 servings.

CORN AND PEPPER BAKE

1 (14¾ ounce) can cream-style corn
½ cup liquid egg substitute
1 tablespoon melted butter
2 tablespoons finely chopped green pepper
2 tablespoons unbleached flour
¼ cup milk
½ teaspoon salt

Preheat oven to 350 degrees. In a large bowl, combine all ingredients. Mix well. In a 9x13 inch baking pan, place ingredients. Bake for 1 hour or until knife inserted in center comes out clean. Makes 6 to 8 servings.

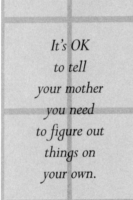

It's OK
to tell
your mother
you need
to figure out
things on
your own.

CORN BROCCOLI AND TOMATO DISH

1 bunch fresh broccoli, cut up
1 cup water
1 (10¾ ounce) can corn soup
½ cup shredded Cheddar cheese
¼ cup milk
1 tablespoon snipped fresh basil
Pepper to taste
1 cup quartered cherry tomatoes

In a 3-quart saucepan, combine broccoli and water. Over high heat, bring to a boil. Reduce heat to low. Cover and cook 8 minutes or until broccoli is tender-crisp, stirring often. Drain in colander. In same saucepan, combine soup, cheese, milk, basil, and pepper. Over medium heat, heat thoroughly, stirring occasionally. Stir in tomatoes and serve. Makes 6 to 8 servings.

BROCCOLI AND PINE NUTS STIR-FRY

1 pound fresh broccoli, cut into flowerets
1 tablespoon butter
3 tablespoons fresh lime juice
¼ cup toasted pine nuts

In a steamer, steam broccoli until tender-crisp, about 2 minutes. Drain and let dry on a paper towel. In a large skillet, melt butter. Add broccoli and lime juice. Stir-fry broccoli for 3 minutes. Just before serving add pine nuts. Makes 2 to 4 servings.

Patience comes from a loving and tender heart.

CAULIFLOWER SUPREME

1 pound cauliflower, steamed
2 tablespoons butter
2 tablespoons bread crumbs
1 egg, boiled and chopped
Salt and pepper to taste
½ teaspoon parsley

In a large serving dish, arrange cauliflower. In a medium skillet, melt butter and add bread crumbs. Fry until lightly brown. Add egg, salt, and pepper. Pour over steamed cauliflower and garnish with parsley. Makes 4 to 6 servings.

DRESSED UP FOR COMPANY SQUASH

2 pounds yellow squash
¼ cup mayonnaise
¼ cup chopped green peppers
½ stick margarine or butter
1 tablespoon sugar
½ cup chopped onions
¼ cup shredded Cheddar cheese
1 egg
Salt and pepper to taste
Buttered bread or cracker crumbs or
  shredded Cheddar cheese for topping

Preheat oven to 350 degrees. In a medium pot, cook squash and drain. Add mayonnaise, peppers, margarine, sugar, onions, cheese, egg, salt, and pepper. Mix well. Pour into buttered 2-quart casserole dish. Top with crumbs or cheese. Bake for 35-40 minutes or until brown. Makes 6 to 8 servings.

When things are going rough that is the time to be tough. Walk in the light of the Lord and He will show you how to make it through.

VEGGIE PEPPERS

4 green or red bell peppers,
  tops and seeds removed
2 tablespoons butter
1/2 cup chopped onions
1 cup fresh or frozen peas
1 large carrot, chopped
1/4 teaspoon salt
1/4 teaspoon pepper
1 cup cooked rice
Cooking spray

Preheat oven to 350 degrees. In a large saucepan, cook peppers in boiling water for 2 minutes. Drain off water and set aside. In a large skillet, melt butter and brown onions, peas, and carrots. Add salt and pepper. Cook until softened. Drain, if necessary, and stir in cooked rice. Stuff peppers with ingredients from the skillet. In a 2½-quart baking dish, lightly coated with cooking spray, place stuffed peppers. Bake for 10 minutes or until heated throughout. Makes 4 servings.

ITALIAN EGGPLANT

3 large eggs, lightly beaten
1½ cups Italian seasoned bread crumbs
1/4 cup olive oil
1 large eggplant, cut crosswise in 1/8 inch
  thick slices
1/4 cup grated Parmesan or Romano cheese

In a medium bowl, place eggs. In another medium bowl, place bread crumbs. In a large skillet pour olive oil and heat. Take eggplant slices one at a time, and dip them in egg and then in bread crumbs. Fry eggplant, 1 to 2 minutes on each side or until golden brown. Drain on paper towel and serve. Place on a plate and sprinkle with cheese. Makes 4 to 6 servings.

Being a family member does not give us the right to become intrusive.

Veggie Fettuccine

8 ounces fettuccine
2 small zucchini, sliced lengthwise, paper thin
2 carrots, sliced lengthwise, paper thin
2 tomatoes, peeled, seeded, and chopped
10 small black olives, pitted and quartered
1 tablespoon extra-virgin olive oil
2 teaspoons shredded Parmesan cheese
1 teaspoon minced pickled hot red pepper
1 garlic clove, minced
Freshly ground pepper to taste

In a large saucepan, cook the fettuccine according to the package directions, after about 8 minutes, add the zucchini and carrots. Cook until the pasta is al dente and the vegetables are tender, 2 to 3 minutes longer. In a large bowl, combine the tomatoes, olives, oil, cheese, red pepper, garlic, and ground pepper in a serving bowl. Drain the pasta and vegetables, and then add to the sauce, tossing to coat. Makes 6 to 8 servings.

Canaan's Pasta Shells

8 ounces pasta shells, cooked and drained
½ stick butter
¼ teaspoon garlic powder
¾ cup shredded Parmesan cheese

In a large serving bowl, place pasta. In a small saucepan, melt butter and garlic. Add to pasta and toss lightly. Add cheese and toss lightly. Serve immediately. Makes 4 to 6 servings.

*Good fortune
is what happens
when opportunity
meets with
preparation.*

Thomas A. Edison

*A*NGEL *H*AIR *C*ARBONARA

⅓ cup milk
1½ cups water
2 tablespoons margarine or butter
1 (4.8 ounce) package angel hair pasta
2 cups cooked, chopped pork or ham
1 (10 ounce) package frozen peas
¼ cup sliced green onions
Salt and pepper to taste

In a round 3-quart microwaveable glass casserole dish,
combine milk, water, and margarine. Microwave,
uncovered, on high 4 to 5 minutes or until boiling.
Gradually add pasta while stirring. Separate pasta with
fork, if needed. Microwave, uncovered, on high 4 minutes,
stirring gently after 2 minutes. Separate pasta with fork,
if needed. Stir in meat, peas, onions, salt, and pepper.
Continue to microwave 2 to 3 minutes. Sauce will be
thin, let stand 3 minutes or until desired consistency.
Stir before serving. Salt and pepper. Makes 4 to 6 servings.

*T*OMATO-GARLIC *A*NGEL *H*AIR *P*ASTA

1 pound package angel hair pasta
3 large ripe tomatoes, peeled, seeded, and chopped
⅓ cup olive or vegetable oil
¼ cup shredded Parmesan cheese
¼ cup minced fresh parsley
1 garlic clove, minced
1 tablespoon minced fresh basil
¼ teaspoon garlic salt

Cook pasta according to package directions. In a large bowl,
combine tomatoes, oil, cheese, parsley, garlic, basil, and
garlic salt. Rinse and drain pasta, add to tomato mixture
and toss to coat. Serve immediately. Makes 6 to 8 servings.

*Remember
your elderly
family members;
you will be
elderly one day.*

ZESTY PASTA

½ pound ground beef, browned,
   crumbled and drained
1 (26½ ounce) jar of garlic and onion
   spaghetti sauce
¼ cup grated Parmesan cheese
¼ teaspoon pepper
1 (10 ounce) package frozen chopped spinach,
   thawed and well drained
4 cups cooked corkscrew macaroni

In a large skillet, combine beef, spaghetti sauce, cheese, and pepper. Bring to a boil. Reduce heat, cover and cook for 5 minutes, stirring occasionally. Stir in spinach and macaroni. Makes 6 to 8 servings.

ELBOW BEEF AND CORN DISH

1 pound ground round
Salt and pepper to taste
1 teaspoon garlic powder
½ cup chopped onions
1 (8 ounce) can tomato sauce
1 cup stewed tomatoes
1 (15.5 ounce) can whole kernel corn, drained
1 cup cooked elbow macaroni
4 tablespoons shredded Parmesan cheese

In a large skillet, brown and crumble ground round. Add salt, pepper, garlic powder, and onions. Cook over medium-high heat. Remove skillet from heat for 2 minutes. Drain grease off. Add sauce, tomatoes, corn, and cooked macaroni. Stir well and allow to heat thoroughly, about 5 to 7 minutes. Sprinkle with cheese. Makes 6 to 8 servings.

Additional problems are offsprings of poor solutions.

Mark Twain

BEEF TOMATOES AND NOODLES

1½ pounds beef stew meat, cubed
¼ cup self-rising flour
2 cups stewed tomatoes
1 teaspoon salt
¼ teaspoon pepper
1 medium onion, chopped
Water
1 (12 ounce) bag noodles, cooked

In a large bowl, cover meat with flour. In a slow cooker, place coated meat, tomatoes, salt, pepper, and onion. Add enough water to cover ingredients. Cover and cook on low for 6 hours. Serve mixture over cooked noodles. Makes 6 to 8 servings.

BEEF BURGUNDY AND NOODLES

5 medium onions, thinly sliced
2 pounds beef stew meat, cubed
1½ tablespoons self-rising flour
½ pound fresh mushrooms
1 teaspoon salt
¼ teaspoon dried thyme
¼ teaspoon dried marjoram
⅛ teaspoon pepper
¼ cup beef broth
1½ cups Burgundy cooking wine
1 (12 ounce) bag noodles, cooked

Preheat oven to 325 degrees. In a roasting pan, place onions. In a large bowl, cover meat with flour and place in roasting pan. Combine mushrooms, salt, thyme, marjoram, and pepper. Pour in broth and wine. Cover and cook for 45 minutes. Serve over noodles. Makes 6 to 8 servings.

Opportunities appear at different times during the day. Keep your eyes open.

BEEFY NOODLE DISH

2 (10¾ ounce) cans condensed tomato soup
2 tablespoons garlic powder
¼ cup shredded Parmesan cheese
8 ounces Cheddar cheese, shredded
1 cup water
6 ounce package noodles, cooked
1 pound ground beef, browned, crumbled
  and drained
¼ cup shredded Parmesan cheese

Preheat oven to 350 degrees. In a large saucepan, combine soup, garlic powder, Parmesan cheese, Cheddar cheese, and water. Mix well. Heat until cheese is melted and a sauce is formed. Add noodles and meat. Mix well. Cover and cook for 3 minutes. In a large serving bowl, pour mixture and sprinkle Parmesan cheese on the top and serve. Makes 6 to 8 servings.

CHEESE LOVERS ZITI

1 pound ziti pasta, cooked
1 pound ground beef, browned, crumbled,
  and drained
6 ounces provolone cheese, sliced
1½ cups sour cream
6 ounces mozzarella cheese, shredded
4 tablespoons shredded Parmesan cheese
2 (26 ounce) jars spaghetti sauce
1 onion, chopped
1 teaspoon butter

Preheat oven to 350 degrees. In a large bowl, combine all ingredients. Mix well. In a 9x13 inch buttered baking pan, pour mixture. Bake uncovered for 20 minutes. Remove from oven and let sit for 5 minutes before serving. Makes 6 to 8 servings.

Children learn by observing those around them.

SKILLET HAMBURGER DINNER

1½ pounds ground beef
½ onion, chopped
1 teaspoon garlic powder
Salt and pepper to taste
1 (8 ounce) can tomato sauce
1 cup stewed tomatoes
1 (15 ounce) can whole kernel corn, drained
1 cup cooked elbow macaroni

In a large skillet, over medium heat, sauté ground beef for 5
minutes. Add onion and sauté for 3 minutes. Season with
garlic powder, salt, and pepper. Combine the tomato sauce,
tomatoes, corn, and cooked macaroni. Stir well. Cook 5 to
7 minutes. Makes 8 to 10 servings.

JIFFY BEEF STROGANOFF

1½ pounds lean ground beef
1 package onion soup mix
1 (16 ounce) package noodles
2½ cups water
1 cup sour cream
1 (15.5 ounce) can English peas

In a large skillet, brown ground beef, stirring until crumbly.
Drain and add soup mix. Mix well. Cover with noodles.
Add enough water to moisten noodles. Simmer, covered,
until noodles are tender. Stir in sour cream and peas. Makes
6 to 8 servings.

Before I got
married
I had six
theories
about raising
children.
Now I have
six children
and no theories.

John Wilmot

SPAGHETTI PIZZA

12 ounces spaghetti, cooked and chopped
2 eggs, beaten
½ cup milk
1 cup shredded mozzarella cheese
Favorite pizza toppings
1 (26 ounce) jar spaghetti sauce
1 pound ground beef, browned and crumbled
3 cups shredded mozzarella cheese

Preheat oven to 400 degrees. In a large bowl, combine spaghetti, eggs, milk, and 1 cup mozzarella cheese. May add olives, mushrooms, onions, and green pepper or other favorite pizza toppings. Mix well. In a 9x13 inch baking pan, spread mixture. Bake at 400 degrees for 15 minutes. Remove from oven and spread with spaghetti sauce. Crumble ground beef over top. Sprinkle with 3 cups mozzarella cheese. Bake at 350 degrees for 30 minutes. Makes 6 to 8 servings.

ONION BEEF AND NOODLES

1 pound round steak, cubed
2 can cream of golden mushroom soup
1 large onion, chopped
1 teaspoon salt
½ teaspoon pepper
¼ teaspoon garlic salt
1 cup water
4 to 6 cups noodles, cooked

In a crock-pot place all ingredients except noodles. Mix well. Cook on low for 8 hours. Serve over noodles. Makes 4 to 6 servings.

Life is hard, but you can draw strength from those around you.

HAM AND MACARONI TWISTS

2 cups cooked rotini
1½ cups cubed, cooked ham
1⅓ cups French fried onions, divided
1 (10 ounce) frozen broccoli spears,
   thawed and drained
1 cup milk
1 (10¾ ounce) can cream of celery soup
1 cup shredded Cheddar cheese, divided
¼ teaspoon garlic powder
¼ teaspoon pepper

Preheat oven to 350 degrees. In a 9x13 inch baking pan,
combine rotini, ham, and ⅔ cup onions. Divide broccoli
spears into 6 small bunches. Arrange bunches of broccoli
down center of dish, alternating direction of flowerets. In
small bowl, combine milk, soup, ½ cup cheese, garlic, and
pepper. Pour mixture over dish. Bake, covered, for 30
minutes or until heated thoroughly. Top with remaining
cheese and ⅔ cup onions, down center. Bake, uncovered,
5 minutes or until golden brown. Makes 4 to 6 servings.

MAKE IT EASY CHICKEN

1 (10¾ ounce) can white meat chicken
1 (10¾ ounce) can cream of chicken soup
2 tablespoons butter
4 cups cooked macaroni

Preheat oven to 350 degrees. In a large bowl, combine
all ingredients. Mix well. In a 2-quart baking dish, pour
mixture. Bake for 10 to 15 minutes. Makes 6 to 8 servings.

*If we could
read the secret
history of
our enemies,
we should find
in each man's life
sorrow and
suffering enough
to disarm
all hostility.*

Henry Wadsworth Longfellow

The **Good Earth**

SCALLOPED CHICKEN & PASTA

2¼ cups water
¼ cup margarine or butter, divided
1 (6.2 ounce) package macaroni shells
¼ cup shredded, melted white Cheddar cheese
2 cups frozen mixed vegetables
⅔ cup milk
2 cups chopped cooked chicken or ham
¼ cup dry bread crumbs

Preheat oven to 450 degrees. In a 3-quart saucepan, combine water and 2 tablespoons margarine. Bring to a boil. Stir in pasta, cheese, and vegetables. Reduce heat to medium. Boil, uncovered, stirring frequently, 12 to 14 minutes or until most of water is absorbed. Add milk and chicken. Continue cooking 3 minutes. In a small saucepan, melt remaining margarine and stir in bread crumbs. In a 9x13 inch baking pan, pour pasta mixture. Sprinkle with bread crumb mixture. Bake 10 minutes or until bread crumbs are browned and edges are bubbly. Makes 4 to 6 servings.

VEGGIE CHICKEN AND SPAGHETTI

2 tablespoons vegetable oil
2 large chicken breasts, cubed
1 (21 ounce) package frozen stir-fry and sauce
2 cups cooked spaghetti

In a large skillet, heat oil. Cook chicken until done. Cook stir-fry with chicken according to package directions. Serve over spaghetti. Makes 2 to 4 servings.

Don't be so busy that you don't have time to listen. Spend time in prayer today and listen. God has something to share with you.

BEEF AND RICE SKILLET DINNER

1 pound ground beef, browned,
    crumbled and drained
1 large onion, chopped
2½ cups water
1 cup uncooked rice
3 beef bouillon cubes, crushed
½ teaspoon dry mustard
1 medium green bell pepper, chopped
1 medium tomato, chopped
1 cup shredded Monterey Jack cheese

In a large skillet, combine beef, onion, water, rice, bouillon, and dry mustard. Bring to a boil over medium heat. Reduce heat, simmer, and cover. Cook for 25 minutes or until liquid is absorbed. Stir in green pepper and tomato. Sprinkle cheese over top. Remove from heat. Let stand, covered, for 2 to 3 minutes or until cheese is melted. Makes 6 to 8 servings.

BEEF STROGANOFF AND RICE

1 tablespoon oil
1 pound stew meat
2 soup cans of milk
½ cup chopped onion
1 (4 ounce) can mushrooms, sliced
1 (10¾ ounce) can cream of mushroom soup
1 (10¾ ounce) can cream of celery soup
¼ teaspoon garlic salt
1 cup sour cream
6 cups cooked rice

In a large skillet, place oil and brown meat. Combine milk, onion, mushrooms, mushroom and celery soups, garlic salt, and sour cream. Cover and cook on low heat for 45 minutes. Stir occasionally. Serve over rice. Makes 4 to 6 servings.

*Man is great
only when
he is kneeling.*

Pope Pius XII

CHICKEN FLAVORED RICE

Cooking spray
2 tablespoons chicken broth
1 cup uncooked rice
¾ cup chopped onion
½ cup sliced green pepper
2 teaspoons chili powder
1 cup crushed tomatoes
2 cups water

Coat a large nonstick skillet with cooking spray. Add chicken broth and heat. Stir in rice and cook until rice is lightly browned. Add onion, green pepper, chili powder, tomatoes, and water. Cover and simmer over low heat 20 to 25 minutes, until all liquid has been absorbed. Makes 2 to 4 servings.

BOUNTIFUL SEAFOOD RICE

½ cup butter or margarine
2 celery stalks, chopped
1 medium red onion, chopped
1 cup long grain rice
2 teaspoons curry
⅛ teaspoon cayenne pepper
2 cups chicken broth
½ pound crab (canned okay)
½ pound tiny shrimp
3 tablespoons parsley
Salt and pepper to taste

In a large pot, melt butter and add celery and onion. Cook until brown (8 minutes). Add rice, curry, and cayenne. Stir until rice is brown. Add broth and bring to boil. Reduce heat. Cover and simmer about 18 minutes (until rice is done). Stir in seafood and parsley. Add salt and pepper. Makes 6 to 8 servings.

Earth is the right place for love. It can only be shared when it is expressed to those around you.

SHEPHERD'S STAFF CASSEROLE

¼ teaspoon vegetable oil
1 pound ground beef, browned,
   crumbled and drained
3 cups creamed potatoes
15 ounces Cheddar cheese, shredded

Preheat oven to 350 degrees. Spread creamed potatoes in a
greased 3-quart casserole dish. Layer with ground beef and
cheese. Bake for 10 minutes or until cheese has melted.
Makes 4 to 6 servings.

GREEN PEPPER CHILI

1 pound ground beef, browned,
   crumbled and drained
1 onion, chopped
1 green pepper, chopped
1½ teaspoons salt
1 tablespoon chili powder
2 tablespoons Worcestershire sauce
3 (15½ ounce) cans kidney beans, drained
1 (14½ ounce) can crushed or stewed tomatoes
2 cups shredded Cheddar cheese

In a large pot, combine beef, onion, green pepper, salt, chili
powder, Worcestershire sauce, beans, and tomatoes. Mix
well. Cook over low heat for 45 minutes. Serve in bowls
and top with cheese. Makes 6 to 8 servings.

*The courage
to accept oneself
can come
from Christ.
He accepted us
even when
we were
unacceptable.*

CHILI AND CHEESE ON RICE

1 pound ground beef
1 onion, diced
1 teaspoon dried basil
1 teaspoon dried oregano
1 (16 ounce) can light red kidney beans
1 (15½ ounce) can chili beans
1 pint stewed tomatoes, drained
4 cups cooked rice
8 ounces Cheddar cheese, shredded

In a large skillet, brown ground beef and onion. Add basil and oregano. In a large saucepan, combine beef, onion, basil, oregano, beans, and tomatoes. Mix well. Cover and cook over low heat for 45 minutes. Serve over cooked rice and top with cheese. Makes 10 to 12 servings.

ROAST BEEF CASSEROLE

1 (8 ounce) jar pasteurized process cheese spread
¾ cup milk
2 cups cooked, cubed roast beef
1 (16 ounce) bag frozen vegetable combination
   (broccoli, corn, red pepper), thawed
4 cups frozen hash brown potatoes, thawed
1⅓ cups French-fried onions, divided
½ teaspoon seasoned salt
¼ teaspoon ground pepper
½ cup shredded Cheddar cheese

Preheat oven to 375 degrees. In a 9x13 inch baking pan, spoon cheese spread. Heat in oven just until processed cheese melts, about 5 minutes. Using a fork, stir milk into melted cheese. Mix well. Stir in beef, vegetables, potatoes, ⅔ cup of French-fried onions, salt, and pepper. Bake covered, for 30 minutes or until heated thoroughly. Top with cheese and sprinkle remaining ⅔ cup French-fried onions down center. Bake uncovered, 3 minutes or until onions are golden brown. Makes 6 to 8 servings.

*I can forgive
but I can not forget
is but another
way of saying,
'I can not forgive'.*

Henry Ward Beecher

Tomato Hamburger Stew

2 pounds ground beef, browned and drained
1/2 cups finely chopped onion
(28 ounce) can tomatoes, chopped
cup picante sauce
(15 ounce) can pinto beans, rinsed, drained
(15.5 ounce) can whole kernel corn, drained
teaspoon cumin
1/2 teaspoon garlic powder
1/2 teaspoon pepper
Salt to taste
1/4 cup shredded Cheddar cheese

In a large skillet, combine ground beef, onion, tomatoes, picante sauce, beans, corn, cumin, garlic powder, pepper, and salt. Simmer, covered, for 15 to 20 minutes. Sprinkle with cheese. Makes 8 to 10 servings.

Quick Beef Skillet Meal

1 pound ground beef
1 small onion, chopped
1 (26 ounce) can spaghetti with tomato sauce
1 (16 ounce) can French-fried potato sticks

In a large skillet, brown ground beef, stirring well. Add onion. Cook over low heat until done. Add spaghetti. Stir until well blended. In a 9x13 inch baking pan, pour mixture. Bake for 30 minutes. Arrange potato sticks over spaghetti. Makes 4 to 6 servings.

*Love is
a strange thing;
the more
you give it
away the
more you have.*

HAMBURGER POTATOES

3 medium potatoes, peeled and sliced
3 carrots, sliced
1 small onion, sliced
2 tablespoons dry rice
½ teaspoon pepper
1 pound ground beef, browned and drained
2 cups tomato juice

Preheat oven to 350 degrees. In a large bowl, combine all ingredients. Mix well. In a 9x13 inch baking pan, pour mixture. Cover and cook on low for 1 hour. Makes 4 to 6 servings.

CAN'T MISS SPICY JOES

1 pound hamburger, browned, crumbled and drained
2 tablespoons onion powder
½ green pepper, cut in small cubes
½ teaspoon Worcestershire sauce
1 small onion, chopped
½ cup ketchup
1 teaspoon mustard
1 teaspoon garlic powder
¼ teaspoon pepper
Bread, pitas, or flour tortillas

In a large skillet, combine all ingredients. Cook over medium-high heat until mixture comes to a boil. Reduce temperature to low, cover and simmer 20 to 30 minutes. Serve over bread, stuffed in pita pockets, or rolled in flour tortillas. Makes 6 to 8 servings.

*Remember who
your friends
are on
the way up
because they
are the
some ones
you will meet
on the way
down.*

Anonymous

HEAVENLY HASH

2 cups sliced onions
¼ cup chopped green bell pepper
3 tablespoons vegetable oil
1 pound lean ground beef
1 (16 ounce) can tomatoes
1 teaspoon salt
1 tablespoon chili powder
½ cup uncooked rice

Preheat oven to 350 degrees. In a large skillet, sauté onions and green pepper in oil until brown. Drain. Stir in ground beef, tomatoes, salt, chili powder, and rice. Mix well. Spoon mixture into greased 9x13 inch baking pan. Bake, covered, at 350 degrees for 1 hour. Makes 6 to 8 servings.

CRUSTY BEEF CASSEROLE

1 pound ground beef, browned,
   crumbled and drained
1 (15.5 ounce) can corn, drained
1 (15 ounce) can pinto beans
1 (7 ounce) package cornbread mix

Preheat oven to 375 degrees. In a 9x13 inch baking pan, combine beef, corn, and beans. Prepare cornbread mix using package directions. Spread over beef mixture. Bake for 35 minutes or until brown. Makes 4 to 6 servings.

Love is not a characteristic of God, God is love.

SWISS HAM AND NOODLE CASSEROLE

2 tablespoons butter
½ cup chopped onions
½ cup chopped green pepper
1 (10¾) ounce can cream of mushroom soup
1 cup sour cream
2 teaspoons butter
1 (8 ounce) package medium noodles,
  cooked and drained
2 cups shredded Swiss cheese
2 cups cubed, cooked ham

Preheat oven to 350 degrees. In a medium saucepan, melt butter. Sauté onions and green pepper. Remove from heat. Stir in soup and sour cream. In buttered 2-quart casserole dish, layer ⅓ of the noodles, ⅓ of the cheese, ⅓ of the ham, and ½ of soup mixture. Repeat layers, ending with final ⅓ layer of noodles, cheese, and ham. Bake for 30 to 45 minutes or until heated thoroughly. Makes 6 to 8 servings.

EASY QUICHE

1 (9 inch) pie shell
1 cup chopped ham
¾ cup shredded Swiss cheese
4 eggs, slightly beaten
1 cup heavy cream
2 tablespoons chopped parsley
⅛ teaspoon nutmeg
Salt and pepper to taste

Preheat oven to 400 degrees. Put ham and cheese in pie shell. In a medium bowl, combine eggs, cream, parsley, nutmeg, salt, and pepper. Mix well. Pour over ham and cheese. Bake for 25 minutes. Makes 6 servings.

*Mud thrown
is ground lost.*

Anonymous

HAM AND CHEESE CASSEROLE

2 (10 ounce) packages frozen chopped broccoli
2 cups cooked, cubed smoked ham
1½ cups shredded Cheddar cheese
1 cup Bisquick®
3 cups milk
4 eggs

Preheat oven to 350 degrees. In a medium saucepan, cook broccoli as directed on package. Drain. In a 9x13 inch baking pan, spread broccoli. Layer ham and cheese over broccoli. In a large bowl, combine Bisquick®, milk, and eggs with an electric mixer until smooth. Slowly pour over cheese. Bake, uncovered, for 1 hour. Makes 6 to 8 servings.

CORN AND SAUSAGE CASSEROLE

¾ pound pork sausage
¼ cup chopped green peppers
2 cups drained whole kernel corn
2 tablespoons self-rising flour
½ teaspoon salt
1 (12 ounce) can evaporated milk
½ cup shredded American cheese
6 tomato slices

Every silver lining has a cloud.

Jenny Brannan

Preheat oven to 350 degrees. In a medium skillet, cook sausage and peppers over medium heat until sausage is thoroughly cooked (8 to10 minutes). In a small bowl, pour 2 tablespoons of meat drippings. In a 1½-quart casserole dish, pour meat, peppers, and add corn. Mix well. In the skillet, pour meat drippings and add flour and salt. Cook over medium heat. Slowly add milk. Simmer 2 to 3 minutes or until thickened. Pour over mixture in casserole dish. Add shredded cheese and tomato slices. Bake for 25 to 30 minutes. Makes 6 to 8 servings.

FAMILY TIME BREAKFAST SAUSAGE

Cooking spray
1 can crescent rolls
1 pound sausage, browned, crumbled and drained
8 ounces mozzarella cheese, shredded
4 eggs
¾ cup milk
Salt and pepper to taste

Preheat oven to 425 degrees. Coat a 9x13 inch baking pan with cooking spray. Spread crescent rolls in bottom of pan. Layer pan with sausage then cheese. In a medium bowl, combine eggs and milk. Add salt and pepper. Pour over layers. Bake 15 to 20 minutes or until cooked thoroughly. Makes 4 to 6 servings.

QUICK CHICKEN STIR-FRY

2 teaspoons olive or vegetable oil, divided
1 pound chicken breast, boneless, skinless, cut into strips
1 medium red pepper, cut into strips
1 medium zucchini, cut lengthwise in half and thinly sliced
8 ounces bean sprouts
½ cup prepared stir-fry sauce

In a large nonstick skillet, heat 1 teaspoon oil over medium-high heat. Cook chicken until done. Remove and set aside. Heat remaining 1 teaspoon oil and cook pepper, zucchini, and sprouts, stirring occasionally, 9 minutes or until tender. Return chicken to skillet and stir in stir-fry sauce. Heat thoroughly. Makes 4 to 6 servings.

There is only one letter difference between danger and anger.

Anonymous

CORNBREAD CHICKEN POT PIE

1 (10¾ ounce) can cream of chicken soup
1 (8 ounce) can whole kernel corn, drained
2 cups cooked, cubed chicken
1 (8½ ounce) corn muffin mix
¾ cup milk
1 egg
½ cup shredded Cheddar cheese

Preheat oven to 400 degrees. In a 9 inch pie plate, combine soup, corn, and chicken. In a separate medium bowl, combine muffin mix, milk, and egg. Mix well. Pour over chicken. Bake for 30 minutes or until golden brown. Sprinkle with cheese. Makes 6 servings.

SOFT CHICKEN TACOS

Cooking spray
1 pound chicken tenders, cut in half
1 tablespoon taco seasoning mix
4 flour tortillas
¼ cup shredded Cheddar cheese
½ cup chunky-style salsa

Lightly coat grill. In a medium bowl, place chicken pieces and seasoning until coated. On metal skewers, thread chicken. Grill for 10 to 15 minutes, until thoroughly cooked. Lightly spray large piece (about 18 inches) foil with cooking spray. Fill each tortilla with ¼ chicken pieces, 1 tablespoon cheese, and 2 tablespoons salsa. Roll up burrito-style and place on foil sheet. Cook on grill 2 to 3 minutes, just until cheese is melted and tacos are heated thoroughly. Makes 4 servings.

Here is a woman that is always tired. She lives in a world where much is required.

Mrs. Winston Churchill

VEGETABLES AND SESAME CHICKEN

2 teaspoons peanut oil
1 pound chicken breast, boneless, skinless,
    cut into bite-size pieces
2 cups broccoli and cauliflower florets
2 tablespoons teriyaki sauce
1 teaspoon sesame oil

In a large skillet or wok, over medium heat until drops of water 'dance' when sprinkled into skillet, add peanut oil into the skillet and swirl to coat. Add chicken and cook until done. Add broccoli and cauliflower. Stir-fry until broccoli turns bright green. Cover skillet and simmer for 5 minutes. Stir in teriyaki sauce and sesame oil and serve. Mix well. Makes 2 to 4 servings.

CHICKEN IN THE FIELD

2 (10¾ ounce) cans cream of mushroom soup
2½ cups milk
1½ cups uncooked white rice
2 (4½ ounce) cans mushrooms, sliced
1 package dry onion soup mix
4 chicken breasts, boneless, skinned

Preheat oven to 350 degrees. In a large mixing bowl, combine cream of mushroom soup with milk. Mix well. Add rice, mushrooms, and soup mix. In a 9x13 inch baking pan, spoon rice mixture. Place the chicken on top. Cover with aluminum foil. Bake for 1 hour. Makes 4 servings.

A tranquil heart is life to the body.

CHICKEN POCKETS

Cooking spray
2 medium carrots, sliced thin
2 medium zucchini, sliced thin
1 pound chicken breasts, boneless, skinless
½ teaspoon garlic powder
1 teaspoon onion powder
½ teaspoon dill weed
½ teaspoon paprika
1 medium lemon, sliced

Preheat oven to 350 degrees. Cut four 12-inch squares of foil and coat with cooking spray. Divide carrot and zucchini slices among foil squares, place chicken on top of vegetables. Sprinkle with garlic powder, onion powder, dill weed, and paprika. Top with lemon slices. Fold foil around chicken and place on baking sheet. Bake for 20 to 30 minutes, until chicken is cooked thoroughly and vegetables are tender. Makes 4 to 6 servings.

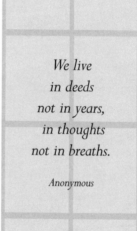

*We live
in deeds
not in years,
in thoughts
not in breaths.*

Anonymous

LEMON BROCCOLI RICE AND CHICKEN

1 tablespoon oil
4 chicken breasts, boneless, skinless,
   cut into strips
1½ cups cooked instant rice
2 cups broccoli florets
½ cup lemon juice
½ cup water

In a large skillet, heat oil and cook chicken until done. Add cooked rice, broccoli, lemon juice, and water to chicken. Mix well. Cover and cook for 5 minutes. Makes 4 to 6 servings.

CHICKEN TOMATO CASSEROLE

1 (10¾ ounce) can cream of mushroom soup
¾ cup picante sauce
¾ cup sour cream
1 tablespoon chili powder
2 medium tomatoes, chopped
3 cups cooked, cubed chicken or turkey
12 (6 inch) corn tortillas, cut into 1-inch pieces
1 cup shredded Cheddar cheese
½ cup green onions for garnish
Picante sauce
Sour cream

Preheat oven to 350 degrees. In a medium bowl, combine soup, picante sauce, sour cream, chili powder, tomatoes, and chicken. In a 2-quart shallow baking dish, arrange half the tortilla pieces. Top with half the chicken mixture. Repeat layers. Sprinkle with cheese. Bake for 40 minutes or until hot. Serve with additional picante sauce and sour cream. Garnish with green onions. Makes 6 to 8 servings.

TURKEY AND BEAN CHILI

1 pound ground turkey, browned
½ cup chopped onions
2 (8 ounce) cans tomato sauce
1 (15 ounce) can kidney beans or pinto beans
1 (1¼ ounce) package chili seasoning
1 cup shredded Cheddar cheese

In a large saucepan, combine turkey, onions, tomato sauce, beans, and seasoning. Bring to a boil, cover and simmer for 10 minutes. Serve in bowls with cheese sprinkled on top of each serving. Makes 6 to 8 servings.

If we do not turn to the Lord for help, we are in danger of receiving information from one or two other places. The surest protection is to go to our Lord, who has promised to guide us into all truth.

Peter Lord

SOUTHWEST TURKEY STEW

Cooking spray
1 pound ground turkey
1¼ cups chunky-style salsa
½ teaspoon onion powder
1 cup drained corn kernels
1 cup rinsed and drained black beans
1 cup canned crushed tomatoes
2 cups chicken broth
1 (4 ounce) can green chiles,
   drained and chopped
Dash cayenne pepper
¼ teaspoon oregano

Preheat oven to 400 degrees. Lightly coat a 9x13 inch
baking pan with cooking spray. In a medium bowl,
combine turkey, ¼ cup salsa, and onion powder. Mix
well. Roll mixture into 1-inch balls. Place in baking pan.
Bake for 20 to 25 minutes, until lightly browned and
cooked thoroughly. In a large saucepan or medium soup
pot, combine corn, beans, tomatoes, chicken broth,
chiles, cayenne pepper, and oregano. Bring mixture to
boil. Reduce heat to medium-low, cook 15 to 20 minutes,
until heated thoroughly. Add turkey meatballs. Cook
over low heat 5 to 10 minutes. Makes 4 to 6 servings.

*Experience
a celebration
of life,
the building
of relationships,
and the
nurturing
of others.*

TURKEY STUFFIN' DIVAN

1¼ cups boiling water
4 tablespoons melted margarine or butter
4 cups herb-seasoned stuffing
2 cups cooked broccoli cuts
2 cups cooked, cubed turkey
1 (10¾ ounce) cream of celery soup
½ cup milk
1 cup shredded Cheddar cheese

Preheat oven to 350 degrees. In a large mixing bowl, combine water and margarine. Add stuffing and mix lightly. In a 2-quart shallow baking dish, spoon in mixture. Arrange broccoli and turkey over stuffing. In a small bowl, combine soup, milk, and ½ cup cheese. Pour over broccoli and turkey. Sprinkle remaining cheese over mixture. Bake for 30 minutes or until hot. Makes 4 to 6 servings.

TURKEY AND RICE CASSEROLE

½ cup chopped onion
¼ cup margarine
1½ pound ground turkey, browned and crumbled
1 teaspoon salt
½ teaspoon pepper
1½ cups sliced mushrooms
1 (10 ounce) can cream of mushroom soup
1 cup buttermilk
3 cups cooked rice

Preheat oven to 350 degrees. In a 9x13 inch baking dish, combine all ingredients. Mix well. Bake for 15 minutes. Makes 8 to 10 servings.

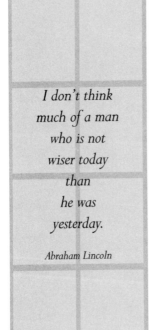

I don't think much of a man who is not wiser today than he was yesterday.

Abraham Lincoln

SOUTHERN SHRIMP CREOLE

Cooking spray
2 tablespoons chicken broth
1/2 cup minced onions
1 clove garlic, crushed
1 1/2 pounds shrimp
1 cup tomato sauce
2 medium tomatoes, peeled and diced
1/2 teaspoon salt
1/8 teaspoon pepper
1/8 teaspoon ground red pepper
Pinch dried oregano
Pinch dried basil
2 cups cooked rice

Coat a large skillet with cooking spray, add chicken broth and heat over medium-high heat. Sauté onions and garlic in broth until soft and lightly browned. Add shrimp and cook 2 to 3 minutes. Stir in tomato sauce, tomatoes, salt, pepper, red pepper, oregano, and basil. Mix well. Reduce heat to low, cover and simmer 15 minutes, until shrimp are pink and cooked thoroughly. Serve over cooked rice. Makes 6 to 8 servings.

DOWN HOME VIDALIA ONION CASSEROLE

4 large Vidalia onions, sliced
1/2 tablespoon margarine
20 townhouse crackers
1 cup shredded Parmesan cheese

Preheat oven to 350 degrees. In a large skillet, place onions and sauté in margarine. In a 1-quart casserole dish, layer onions, crackers, and cheese, repeat layers. Bake for 30 minutes. Makes 4 to 6 servings.

We can't do really big things every day. We have to focus on the small stuff.

Eric Harvey and
Alexander Lucia

SATISFYING POTATO CASSEROLE

3 pounds potatoes, cooked, peeled and diced
16 ounces American cheese, shredded
1 cup real mayonnaise
½ cup chopped onion
½ pound bacon, cooked crisp and crumbled
Salt and pepper to taste

Preheat oven to 350 degrees. In a large mixing bowl, combine potatoes, cheese, mayonnaise, and onion. Mix well. In a 9x13 inch baking pan, pour mixture. Top with bacon. Bake for one hour. Salt and pepper. Makes 4 to 6 servings.

MASHED CHEDDAR CREAM POTATO BAKE

1 (10¾ ounce) can Cheddar cheese soup
⅓ cup sour cream or plain yogurt
Pepper to taste
1 green onion, chopped
3 cups seasoned creamed potatoes

Preheat oven to 350 degrees. In a 1½-quart casserole dish, combine soup, sour cream, pepper, and onion. Stir in potatoes. Bake 30 minutes or until hot all the way through. Makes 2 to 4 servings.

Often time is hard to find. We need to find ways to manage the resource of time or we won't get anything done. We can always make time for the things we love.

HASH BROWN CASSEROLE

2 pounds frozen hash browns, thawed
2 tablespoons minced onion
1 (10¾ ounce) can cream of chicken soup
1 pint sour cream
Salt and pepper to taste
2 cups shredded American cheese
½ cup margarine
2 cups crushed corn flakes

Preheat oven to 350 degrees. In a 2-quart casserole dish, combine hash browns, onion, chicken soup, sour cream, salt, pepper, and cheese. In a small saucepan, melt margarine. Add crushed corn flakes and sprinkle on top of mixture. Bake for 45 minutes. Serve hot. Makes 6 to 8 servings.

SWEET POTATO CASSEROLE

1 pound sweet potatoes, cooked and creamed
2 tablespoons sugar
2 eggs
½ cup whole milk
1 teaspoon vanilla extract
Cooking spray
¼ cup packed brown sugar
2 tablespoons self-rising flour
1 tablespoon butter

Preheat oven to 400 degrees. In a large bowl, place sweet potatoes, sugar, eggs, milk, and vanilla extract. Coat a 1-quart casserole dish with cooking spray. Place mixture in casserole dish. In a medium bowl, combine brown sugar and flour. Sprinkle over sweet potato mixture. Spoon small amounts of butter over the top. Bake for 30 minutes or until brown. Makes 6 to 8 servings.

There is no music in a "rest," but there's the making of music in it.

Ruskin

VEGETARIAN CHILI

3 garlic cloves, minced
2 onions, chopped
1 (16 ounce) can beans of choice, drained
1 green bell pepper, chopped
1 jalapeno pepper, seeds removed, chopped
1 (28 ounce) can diced Italian tomatoes
1 bay leaf
1 tablespoon dried oregano
1 teaspoon salt
¼ teaspoon pepper

In a large pot, combine all ingredients. Mix well. Cover and cook over low heat for 1 hour. Makes 6 to 8 servings.

SESAME HONEY VEGETABLE CASSEROLE

1 (16 ounce) package frozen mixed vegetable
   medley, such as baby carrots, broccoli, onions,
   and red peppers, thawed and drained
3 tablespoons honey
1 tablespoon dark sesame oil
1 tablespoon soy sauce
2 teaspoons sesame seeds

Preheat oven to 350 degrees. In a 1½-quart casserole dish, place vegetables. In a large mixing bowl, combine honey, oil, sauce, and seeds. Mix well. Drizzle evenly over vegetables. Bake for 20 to 25 minutes or until vegetables are hot. Makes 4 to 6 servings.

If it's to be,
it's up to me.

Sharon McFall

BROCCOLI CASSEROLE

Cooking spray
2 (10 ounce) packages frozen chopped broccoli,
  cooked and drained
2 cups sour cream
1 envelope onion soup mix
¼ cup shredded Cheddar cheese

Preheat oven to 350 degrees. Coat a 1-quart casserole dish
with cooking spray. In a medium bowl, combine broccoli,
sour cream, and onion soup mix and mix well. Spread
broccoli mixture into casserole dish. Sprinkle with cheese.
Bake for 30 minutes. Makes 4 to 6 servings.

GREEN BEAN CASSEROLE

2 (14½ ounce) cans green beans, drained
1 (10¾ ounce) can cream of mushroom soup
1 (4 ounce) can French-fried onions

Preheat oven to 350 degrees. In a greased 2-quart casserole
dish pour beans. Spoon soup evenly over beans. Stir to allow
soup to seep into lower part of casserole. Bake uncovered
for 20 minutes. Remove beans from the oven and top with
French-fried onions. Makes 4 to 6 servings.

*It is better
to remain
silent and
be thought a fool,
than to open
your mouth
and remove
all doubt.*

Anonymous

SUPER CREAM-STYLE CORN CASSEROLE

1 (15 ounce) can whole kernel corn
1 (15 ounce) can cream-style corn
1 stick margarine, melted
1 (8 ounce) carton sour cream
1 (6 ounce) package jalapeno cornbread mix

Preheat oven to 350 degrees. In a large bowl, combine all ingredients together. Pour ingredients. In a greased 9x13 inch baking pan. Makes 6 to 8 servings.

GARDEN BAKE CASSEROLE

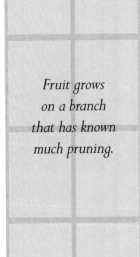

*Fruit grows
on a branch
that has known
much pruning.*

1 cup chopped zucchini
1 cup chopped tomato
½ cup chopped onions
⅓ cup shredded Parmesan cheese
1 cup milk
2 eggs
½ cup Bisquick®
½ teaspoon salt
¼ teaspoon pepper
Tomato and zucchini slices

Preheat oven to 400 degrees. Grease 9 inch pie plate and sprinkle zucchini, tomato, onions, and cheese in plate. In a large bowl, combine milk, eggs, Bisquick®, salt, and pepper. Beat until smooth. Pour into pie plate. Bake until knife inserted in center comes out clean, about 35 to 45 minutes. Cool 5 minutes. Garnish with tomato and zucchini slices if desired. Makes 4 to 6 servings.

Wilderness
Manna

A Friend

6 cups trustworthiness

4 cups confidentiality

1 cup good humor

1 cup sympathy

1 cup hope

2 cups love

4 cups patience

1 strong shoulder to lean on

1 good listening ear

BREADS

BISCUITS

ROLLS

MAMA'S CORNBREAD

1 cup white or yellow cornmeal
3 tablespoons self-rising flour
½ teaspoon salt
1 egg
¾ cup whole milk

Preheat oven to 425 degrees. In a large bowl, combine all ingredients. Mix well. Do not beat. Pour mixture into an 8x8 inch baking pan ¾ full. Bake for 25 minutes or until brown. Makes 6 to 8 servings.

CORNBREAD STICKS

2 tablespoons margarine
½ cup cornmeal
2 tablespoons self-rising flour
1 tablespoon sugar
½ teaspoon salt
1 egg
½ cup whole milk

Preheat oven to 450 degrees. In an iron cornbread stick pan, melt margarine. In a large bowl, combine cornmeal, flour, sugar, salt, egg, and milk. Mix well. Spoon mixture into pan. Bake 8 to 10 minutes or until brown on top. Makes 6 to 8 servings.

Faith —
makes all
things possible,

Hope —
makes all
things bright,

Love -
makes all things
a little easier.

FRIED CORNBREAD

½ cup self-rising cornmeal
⅛ teaspoon salt
½ cup water
1 teaspoon melted butter
1 teaspoon vegetable oil

In a large bowl, combine cornmeal, salt, water, and butter. Mix well. In a large skillet, heat vegetable oil. Drop mixture by spoonfuls into hot grease. Fry both sides until brown. Makes 6 to 8 servings.

BROCCOLI CORNBREAD

2 cups cornmeal
4 eggs
2 (8 ounce) sticks margarine, melted
1 cup cottage cheese
1 medium onion, chopped
1 (8 ounce) package frozen chopped broccoli, drained
1 teaspoon all-purpose flour

Preheat oven to 350 degrees. In a large bowl, combine cornmeal, eggs, margarine, cottage cheese, onion, and broccoli. Pour mixture into greased and floured 9x13 inch baking pan. Bake for 30 to 35 minutes. Makes 6 to 8 servings.

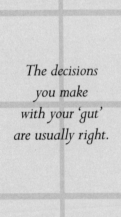

The decisions you make with your 'gut' are usually right.

HUSH PUPPIES

1 cup white cornmeal
1½ teaspoons salt
½ cup chopped onion
1 egg
¼ cup milk
½ cup oil

In a medium bowl, combine cornmeal, salt, onion, egg, and milk. Mix well. In a large skillet, pour oil and heat until hot. Shape mixture into balls and fry until golden brown. Makes 6 to 8 servings.

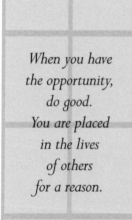

When you have the opportunity, do good. You are placed in the lives of others for a reason.

CHEESY MUFFINS

¾ cup butter
8 ounces sharp or mild Cheddar cheese, grated
1 cup sour cream
2 cups self-rising flour

Preheat oven to 375 degrees. In a large saucepan, melt butter and cheese. Mix well. Cook over medium heat for 2 minutes. Add sour cream. Stir well. Add flour and blend thoroughly. In muffin pans, place paper liners, fill liners ¾ full. Bake for 10 to 12 minutes, or until golden. Makes 4 to 6 servings.

BLUEBERRY CINNAMON MUFFINS

1 cup all-purpose flour
1 tablespoon baking powder
½ teaspoon salt
⅓ cup packed light brown sugar
1 egg
¾ cup milk
3 tablespoons oil
2 teaspoons cinnamon
1 cup blueberries

Preheat oven to 375 degrees. In a large bowl, combine flour, baking powder, salt, sugar, egg, milk, oil, and cinnamon. Mix well. Fold in blueberries. In a muffin pan, place paper liners, fill liners ¾ full. Bake for 25 minutes or until brown. Makes 6 to 8 servings.

HEARTWARMING APPLE MUFFINS

1 cup sugar
3 tablespoons butter
½ teaspoon salt
2 eggs
¾ cup whole milk
1 teaspoon vanilla
2½ cups all-purpose flour
1 teaspoon baking soda
3 cups chopped apples
Cooking spray

Preheat oven to 350 degrees. In a large bowl, cream sugar and butter. Stir in salt, eggs, milk, vanilla, flour, and soda. Mix well. Fold in apples with mixture. In muffin pan, place paper liners, fill liners ¾ full. Bake for 20 minutes. Makes 8 servings.

*Faith is
to believe
what we do not see,
and the reward
of this faith
is to see what
we believe.*

St. Augustine

GOOD FOR YOU MUFFINS

2 cups one-minute oatmeal
2 cups shredded wheat
2 cups all-bran cereal
1 cup boiling water
1 cup vegetable oil
4 eggs, beaten
1 quart buttermilk
1 (1 pound) box brown sugar
4 cups all-purpose flour
5 teaspoons baking soda
1 teaspoon salt
½ cup raisins
½ cup chopped pecans or walnuts

In a large bowl, combine oatmeal, wheat, bran cereal, and water. Mix well. Add oil, eggs, buttermilk, and sugar. Mix well. In a medium bowl, combine flour, soda, and salt. Mix well. Combine flour mixture and cereal mixture. Mix well. Store in refrigerator in plastic container. Use as needed. Add raisins and/or nuts when ready to bake, if desired. Mixture will keep up to 3 months in refrigerator. When ready to bake, preheat oven to 400 degrees. In muffin pan, place paper liners, fill liners ⅔ full. Bake for 12 to 15 minutes. Makes 12 to 14 servings.

Have you had
a kindness shown?
Pass it on;
'twas not given
for thee alone,
pass it on;
let it travel
down the years,
let it wipe
another's tears,
till in heaven
the deed appears —
pass it on.

Henry Burton

Bacon and Cheddar Muffins

2 cups Bisquick®
⅔ cup milk
¼ cup vegetable oil
1 egg
1 cup shredded Cheddar cheese
½ pound bacon, browned, crumbled and drained

Preheat oven to 400 degrees. In a large bowl, combine Bisquick®, milk, vegetable oil, and egg. Mix well. Fold in cheese and bacon just until moistened. In a 12-count muffin pan, place paper liners, fill liners ¾ full. Bake for 20 minutes. Makes 12 servings.

Sunburst Muffins

1 box lemon supreme cake mix
1 (4 serving) box instant lemon pudding
½ cup vegetable oil
1 cup buttermilk
4 eggs

Preheat oven to 350 degrees. In a large bowl, combine all ingredients. Mix well. In miniature muffin pans, place paper liners, fill liners ¾ full. Bake 10 minutes. Makes 20 to 25 servings.

A cheerful heart has a continual feast.

MORNING GLORY MUFFINS

4 cups all-purpose flour
2½ cups sugar
4 teaspoons baking soda
4 teaspoons ground cinnamon
1 teaspoon salt
4 cups coarsely grated carrots
1 cup raisins
1 cup chopped pecans
1 cup flaked coconut
2 tart apples, peeled and grated
6 large eggs
2 cups vegetable oil
2 teaspoons vanilla extract

Preheat oven to 350 degrees. In a large bowl, sift together flour, sugar, baking soda, cinnamon, and salt. Combine carrots, raisins, pecans, coconut, and apples. Set aside. In a medium bowl, whisk together eggs, oil, and vanilla. Add to flour mixture. Mix well. In muffin pans, place paper liners, fill liners ¾ full. Bake for 25 minutes. Makes 30 servings. These freeze very well.

Gather the crumbs of happiness and they will make you a loaf of contentment.

Anonymous

SWEET POTATO MUFFINS

½ cup butter
1¼ cups sugar
2 eggs
1¼ cups cooked and mashed sweet potatoes
1½ cups all-purpose flour
2 teaspoons baking powder
¼ teaspoon salt
1 teaspoon cinnamon
¼ teaspoon nutmeg
1 cup milk
¼ cup chopped pecans or walnuts
½ cup chopped raisins

Preheat oven to 400 degrees. In a large bowl, cream butter and sugar. Add eggs. Mix well. Blend in sweet potatoes. In a medium bowl, sift the flour with the baking powder, salt, cinnamon, and nutmeg. Add flour mixture and milk. Do not over mix. Fold in nuts and raisins. In muffin pans, place paper liners, fill liners ⅔ full. Bake for 25 minutes. Makes 20 servings.

ITALIAN GARLIC BREAD

7 tablespoons butter
4 garlic cloves, crushed
¾ tablespoon olive oil
1 loaf Italian bread
1 cup grated fresh Parmesan cheese

Preheat oven to 350 degrees. In a small bowl, combine butter, garlic, and olive oil. Cut bread into 1-inch slices, almost all the way through, leaving the loaf whole. Brush mixture in-between slices. Place loaf in aluminum foil and twist ends. Sprinkle top with cheese. Bake until tops are bubbly and browned lightly. Makes 8 to 12 servings.

*Children are
gifts from
the Lord;
treat them
with loving care.*

PARTY BREAD

1 pound round sourdough bread, unsliced
1 pound Monterey Jack cheese, sliced
½ cup melted butter
½ cup chopped green onions
3 tablespoons poppy seed

Preheat oven to 350 degrees. Cut bread lengthwise without cutting through to the bottom crust. Insert cheese between the cuts. Combine butter, onions, and poppy seeds. Drizzle over bread. Wrap in foil. Place on a baking sheet. Bake for 15 minutes. Uncover and bake another 10 minutes longer or until the cheese is melted. Makes 8 servings.

CHEWY BREAD

1 (8 ounce) stick margarine
3 eggs
1 (16 ounce) box brown sugar
1 cup chopped nuts
2 cups self-rising flour
1 teaspoon vanilla

Preheat oven to 350 degrees. In a large bowl, cream margarine and eggs. Add sugar, nuts, flour, and vanilla. Mix well. In a 9x13 inch baking pan, pour mixture. Bake for 30 minutes. Makes 6 to 8 servings.

The service we render to others is really the rent we pay for our room on this earth.

Sir Wilfred Grenfell

POPPY SEED BREAD

1 box yellow cake mix
1 (4 serving) box instant vanilla pudding
1 teaspoon almond extract
4 eggs
½ cup vegetable oil
2 tablespoons poppy seed
1 cup hot water
Cooking spray

Preheat oven to 350 degrees. In a large bowl, combine all ingredients, but cooking spray. Mix well. Coat 2 large or 4 small loaf pans with cooking spray, fill pans ¾ full. Bake for 25 to 30 minutes until brown. Makes 8 to 10 servings.

FRUIT BREAD

2¾ cups all-purpose flour
2 cups sugar
1 teaspoon soda
1 teaspoon cinnamon
1 teaspoon salt
1 cup vegetable oil
3 eggs, slightly beaten
2 medium ripe bananas, mashed
1 (8 ounce) can crushed pineapple, undrained
1 (8 ounce) jar maraschino cherries, drained
1 cup chopped pecans
½ cup flaked coconut
1 teaspoon vanilla

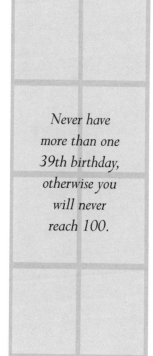

Never have more than one 39th birthday, otherwise you will never reach 100.

Preheat oven to 325 degrees. In a large bowl, sift flour, sugar, soda, cinnamon, and salt. Combine oil, eggs, bananas, pineapple, cherries, pecans, coconut, and vanilla. Mix well. Pour ingredients into greased bread or bundt pan. Bake for 1½ hours. Makes 8 to 10 servings.

SPICY APPLESAUCE BREAD

Cooking spray
1 cup applesauce
1 box yellow cake mix
½ teaspoon cinnamon
1 (4 serving) box instant vanilla pudding
½ teaspoon nutmeg
½ cup raisins

Preheat oven to 350 degrees. Coat two small 5x7 inch loaf pans. In a large bowl, combine applesauce, cake mix, cinnamon, pudding mix, and nutmeg. With an electric mixer, beat on high for 4 minutes. Fold in raisins. Pour mixture into pans. Bake for 35 minutes. Cool in pans for 15 minutes. Makes 8 to 12 servings.

APPLE ROLY POLY

2 cups biscuit mix
½ cup honey
¾ teaspoon cinnamon
¼ teaspoon cloves
3 tablespoons sugar
5 large tart apples, peeled,
**   cored and finely chopped**
1 tablespoon butter
Whipped cream

Preheat oven to 350 degrees. In a large bowl, prepare biscuit mix according to directions. On lightly floured board, roll dough into oblong ¼ inch piece. Spread with honey to within 1 inch of the edges of the dough. In a large bowl, combine cinnamon, cloves, sugar, and apples. Mix well. Spread apple mixture evenly over the honey. Dot apples with butter. Roll up like a jelly roll and seal well. Place rolls onto greased baking sheet, bake for 40 minutes. Slice and serve hot with whipped cream. Makes 6 to 8 servings.

The grass next door may look greener, but it is just as hard to cut.

CRANBERRY BREAD

2 cups all-purpose flour
1 cup sugar
1½ teaspoons baking powder
½ teaspoon baking soda
1 teaspoon salt
1 cup halved cranberries
¼ cup margarine
½ cup chopped pecans
1 egg
¾ cup pineapple juice
Cooking spray

Preheat oven to 350 degrees. In a large bowl, combine all ingredients. Mix well. Pour ingredients into sprayed loaf pan. Bake for 1 hour. Makes 6 to 8 servings.

OATMEAL BREAD

⅓ cup powdered nonfat milk
½ cup quick-cooking oats
3 teaspoons sugar
1 teaspoon cinnamon
¼ teaspoon baking soda
¼ teaspoon cream of tartar
⅓ cup crushed pineapple
Cooking spray

Preheat oven to 325 degrees. In a large bowl, combine all ingredients. Mix well. Pour ingredients into sprayed loaf pan. Bake for 20 minutes. Makes 6 to 8 servings.

*Understanding
is a fountain
of life
to the person
who has it.*

171

THE BEST BANANA BREAD

4 tablespoons butter
4 tablespoons yogurt
1 cup sugar
2 eggs
1½ cups all-purpose flour
1 teaspoon baking soda
1 teaspoon salt
3 very ripe bananas, mashed
1 cup sour cream
1 teaspoon vanilla extract

Preheat oven to 350 degrees. Spray 9x5x3 inch loaf pan. In a large bowl, cream butter, yogurt, and sugar until light and fluffy. Add eggs and beat well. Sift together flour, baking soda, and salt. Combine with the butter mixture. Blend well. Add bananas, sour cream, and vanilla. Mix well. Pour into loaf pan. Bake for 1 hour. Makes 6 to 8 servings.

FAMILY FAVORITE BANANA NUT BREAD

2 bananas, mashed
1 cup sugar
1½ cups all-purpose flour
1 teaspoon baking soda
1 stick butter
2 eggs
½ cup pecans or walnuts
½ teaspoon salt

Preheat oven to 350 degrees. In a large bowl, combine all ingredients. Mix well. Pour into greased loaf pan. Bake for 1 hour. Makes 6 to 8 servings.

*Patience
is idling
your motor
when you feel
like stripping
your gears.*

Anonymous

ORANGE NUT BREAD

1 medium-sized orange
Boiling water
1 cup sliced dates
2 tablespoons salad oil
1 teaspoon vanilla extract
1 egg, beaten
2 cups sifted all-purpose flour
1 cup sugar
1 teaspoon baking soda
½ teaspoon salt
½ cup chopped walnuts or pecans
1 tablespoon shredded orange rind

Preheat oven to 350 degrees. In a measuring cup, squeeze juice from the orange, add boiling water to equal 1 cup. In a large bowl, place dates. Pour orange juice and boiling water over the dates. Add salad oil. Add vanilla and egg. Sift together flour, sugar, baking soda, and salt. Add nuts and orange rind. Mix well. Pour mixture into greased and floured 5x9 inch loaf pan. Bake for 1 hour. Makes 6 to 8 servings.

Love sought is good, but giv'n unsought is better.

William Shakespeare

AUNT FAY'S CINNAMON BREAD

1 egg
½ cup sugar
1 teaspoon cinnamon
¾ cup milk
3 tablespoons butter, melted
½ teaspoon salt
4 tablespoons baking powder
2 cups wheat flour

Preheat oven to 400 degrees. In a large bowl, combine all ingredients. Beat until well blended. Pour into greased 5x9 inch loaf pan. Bake for 20 minutes. Makes 8 to 10 servings.

RISE 'N SHINE COFFEE BREAD

⅓ cup milk
1 egg
¼ cup sugar
2¼ cups Bisquick®
Cooking spray
⅓ cup packed brown sugar
3 tablespoons margarine
1 teaspoon cinnamon
¼ cup nuts

*Love
takes compassion
and puts it
into action.*

Preheat oven to 375 degrees. In a small bowl, combine milk and egg. Mix well. Add sugar and Bisquick®. Mix well. Pour mixture into 8-inch square sprayed baking pan. In a medium bowl, combine brown sugar, margarine, cinnamon, and nuts. Sprinkle mixture on top of bread mix. Bake for 25 minutes. Makes 6 servings.

VANILLA COFFEE BREAD

1 box yellow cake mix
2 (4 serving) boxes instant vanilla pudding
4 eggs
2 teaspoons vanilla
½ cup vegetable oil
1 cup water

TOPPING
½ cup packed brown sugar
½ cup chopped nuts
1 teaspoon sugar

Preheat oven to 300 degrees. In a large bowl, combine cake mix, pudding, eggs, vanilla, oil, and water, for bread. Mix well. In a small bowl, combine brown sugar, nuts, and sugar, for topping. Mix well. Pour half of batter into greased tube pan. Top with half of topping mixture. Pour remaining batter in pan and top with remaining topping. Bake for 40 to 45 minutes. Makes 10 to 12 servings.

FRENCH BREAKFAST PUFFS

⅓ cup shortening
½ cup sugar
1 egg
1½ cups all-purpose flour
1½ teaspoons baking powder
½ teaspoon salt
¼ teaspoon nutmeg
½ cup milk
6 tablespoons melted butter
½ cup sugar
1 teaspoon cinnamon

Preheat oven to 350 degrees. In a large bowl, combine shortening, sugar, and egg until smooth. Add flour, baking powder, salt, and nutmeg. Mix well. Add milk. Mix well. In muffins pans, place paper liners. Fill liners ¾ full with mixture. Bake 20 to 25 minutes. In a small bowl, place melted butter. In a small bowl, combine sugar and cinnamon. Mix well. Remove puffs from oven and immediately dip in butter and sugar mixture. Makes 6 to 8 servings.

ROLLED STRAWBERRY TREATS

1 tube crescent rolls
1½ cups strawberry pie filling
½ cup packed brown sugar

Unroll crescent rolls. Place 2 tablespoons strawberry pie filling in center of each roll. Roll up dough. Sprinkle with brown sugar. Place on a baking sheet. Bake according to directions on crescent packaging. Makes 4 to 6 servings.

*Kindness
is the sign of
greatness.*

Lloyd Ogilvie

POPPY SEED PULL-APARTS

3 tablespoons melted margarine
2 teaspoons dill seed
1 teaspoon poppy seed
¼ teaspoon celery seed
1 (10 ounce) can large biscuits
¼ cup grated Parmesan cheese

Preheat oven to 400 degrees. In a 9-inch cake pan, pour margarine. Sprinkle all seeds over melted margarine. Separate dough into biscuits. Cut each biscuit into 4 pieces. In a bag, place biscuit pieces and cheese. Shake to coat. Arrange pieces evenly in pan, sprinkle on remaining cheese. Bake for 15 to 18 minutes. Makes 6 to 8 servings.

EASY CINNAMON TOAST

1 slice white bread
1 teaspoon butter
½ teaspoon cinnamon sugar

Toast bread. Spread with butter. Sprinkle with sugar. Makes 1 serving.

*A joyful heart
makes a
cheerful face.*

CINNAMON FRENCH TOAST

Cooking spray
¼ cup packed brown sugar
1 teaspoon cinnamon
3 tablespoons melted margarine
¾ cup beaten eggs
2 tablespoons milk
½ teaspoon vanilla
2 teaspoons sugar
8 slices French bread
Confectioners' sugar, syrup, or preserves

Preheat oven to 400 degrees. Lightly coat a 10x15 inch baking pan with cooking spray. In a small bowl, combine brown sugar and cinnamon. Mix well. Spread brown sugar mixture in bottom of dish. Drizzle margarine over sugar. Mix well. In a medium bowl, combine eggs, milk, vanilla, and sugar. Blend until smooth. Dip bread slices in egg mixture and coat on both sides. Arrange slices in baking pan. Pour remaining egg mixture on top. Chill until ready to bake. Bake 20 minutes. Serve with confectioners' sugar, syrup, or preserves. Makes 4 servings.

FRIED BREAD

2 cups flour
1½ teaspoon sugar
½ teaspoon milk
4 teaspoons baking powder
½ cup vegetable oil

In a large bowl, combine flour, sugar, and baking powder. Pour in milk. Mix well. Roll mixture out on a floured board. Cut into 2x4 inch pieces. Score down center of each piece. In a large skillet, heat oil and fry until golden brown. Makes 4 to 6 servings.

It is easy to open your door to welcome a well-loved friend; it is a great gift of hospitality and a test of brotherly love to open the same door to strangers. They can become your friends.

FAMILY FUN HOMEMADE PRETZELS

1½ cups warm water
1 tablespoon sugar
1 tablespoon salt
1 (¼ ounce) package yeast
4 cups all-purpose flour
1 egg

Preheat oven to 425 degrees. In a large bowl, combine water, sugar, salt, and yeast. Mix well. Let sit for 2 to 3 minutes. Add flour to bowl and knead flour. Using small balls of dough, shape dough into anything you like – letters, numbers, or twists. Place dough on a baking sheet. Allow the shapes to sit for 20 to 25 minutes. In a small bowl, beat egg. Brush egg lightly onto shapes. Bake in oven for 12 to 15 minutes. Servings depend on size of shapes.

LIGHT AND FLUFFY PANCAKE BATTER

2 cups pre-sifted all-purpose flour
1 tablespoon baking powder
1 cup nonfat milk
1 teaspoon salt
2 cups milk
1 egg
⅓ cup oil

In a large bowl, combine flour, baking powder, nonfat milk, and salt. Combine milk, egg, and oil. Mix only until all dry ingredients are moist. In a large skillet, cover with oil. Fry pancakes until golden brown. Makes 4 to 6 servings.

Blessed is she who serves laughter and smiles with every meal, for her cheerfulness is an aid to mental and physical digestion.

APPLE PANCAKES

2 cups all-purpose flour
4½ tablespoons sugar
4 teaspoons baking powder
1 teaspoon salt
2 eggs
1¼ cups milk
½ cup apple pie filling
1 stick margarine, melted

In a large bowl, sift flour, sugar, baking powder, and salt.
Combine eggs, milk, and apples. Mix well. On a large grill
or skillet, melt 1 tablespoon margarine. Combine remaining
margarine in batter. Mix well. Makes 6 to 8 servings.

OH BOY WAFFLES

2 cups pre-sifted all-purpose flour
1 tablespoon baking powder
1 teaspoon salt
1½ cups milk
1 egg
⅓ cup oil

In a large bowl, combine flour, baking powder, and salt.
In a medium bowl, combine milk, egg, and oil. Add to
dry ingredients. Mix only until all dry ingredients are
moist. In waffle iron, pour batter. Cook until brown.
Makes 6 to 8 servings.

*What makes the
Dead Sea dead?
Because it is all
the time receiving
but never giving
anything out.*

Dwight L. Moody

ANGEL BISCUITS

5 cups all-purpose flour
1 teaspoon salt
1 teaspoon soda
1 teaspoon sugar
3 teaspoons baking powder
1 (¼ ounce) package dry yeast
½ cup water
¾ cup cooking oil
2 cups buttermilk

Preheat oven to 400 degrees. In a large bowl, sift flour, salt, soda, sugar, and baking powder. In a small bowl, dissolve yeast in warm water. Add oil, buttermilk, and yeast to dry ingredients. Mix well and knead several times, adding flour as needed. Dough will be sticky. Roll out the dough and cut into biscuits. (They do not need to rise first.) Place biscuits onto greased baking sheet. Bake until nicely browned. Keep an eye on them - it takes about 10 minutes. Makes 10 to 12 servings.

IN A PINCH BISCUITS

2 sticks butter
1 cup sour cream
2 cups self-rising flour

Preheat oven to 400 degrees. In a small saucepan, melt butter and cool. In a medium bowl, combine butter, sour cream, and flour. Pour batter into greased miniature muffin pans. Bake 20 minutes. Makes 10 to 12 servings.

Take responsibility on your shoulders and it will leave no room for chips.

ANY OCCASION BISCUITS

1 teaspoon butter
2 cups pre-sifted all-purpose flour
1 tablespoon baking powder
1 teaspoon salt
1 cup milk
⅓ cup oil

Preheat oven to 400 degrees. In a small saucepan, melt 1 teaspoon butter, remove from heat and pour into a biscuit pan. In large bowl, combine flour, baking powder, and salt. Combine milk and oil and add to dry ingredients. Mix only until all dry ingredients are moist. Flour hands with a small amount of flour. Spoon large spoonful of dough into hands and gently form into biscuit shape, the less handling the better. Place biscuit in buttered pan, turn onto opposite side. Bake for about 15 minutes or until browned on top. Makes 6 to 8 servings.

EASY FIX'N BISCUITS

2 cups self-rising flour
½ teaspoon salt
3½ tablespoons shortening
1 cup milk

Preheat oven to 375 degrees. In a large bowl, combine flour and salt. Mix well. Cut in shortening and add milk. Mix well. Drop by spoonfuls onto greased baking sheet. Bake for 15 minutes. Makes 6 to 8 servings.

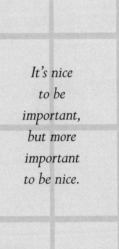

It's nice to be important, but more important to be nice.

BACHELOR BISCUITS

2 cups self-rising flour
⅔ cup mayonnaise
1 cup milk
4 ounces butter

Preheat oven to 350 degrees. In a large bowl, combine flour, mayonnaise, and milk. Mix well. Place a pat of butter in each unit of muffin pan. Pour batter to top of each unit. Bake for 20 minutes. Makes 6 to 8 servings.

WHEAT BISCUITS

2 cups whole wheat flour
4 teaspoons baking powder
½ teaspoon salt
⅓ cup unrefined vegetable oil
1 cup water or milk

Preheat oven to 450 degrees. In a large bowl, combine flour, baking powder, salt, and oil. Add enough water or milk to make a soft dough that is not sticky. Mix just enough to moisten dry ingredients. Pat out dough by hand to ¾ inch thickness on floured board. Cut with a glass. Place biscuits onto greased baking sheet. Bake for 20 minutes. Makes 6 to 8 servings.

When you first woke up this morning, if you did not see Jesus you have already missed a blessing.

FLUFFY BUTTERMILK BISCUITS

2 cups self-rising flour
1½ teaspoons baking powder
1½ teaspoons sugar
⅓ cup shortening
1 cup buttermilk

Preheat oven to 375 degrees. In a large bowl, combine flour, baking powder, and sugar. Mix well. With a fork or pastry blender, cut shortening into mixture. Add buttermilk, stirring until dry ingredients are moistened. Turn dough onto lightly floured cloth. Knead lightly 3 to 4 times. Press out with hands to ½ inch thickness. Cut with a 2½ inch biscuit cutter. Place biscuits onto greased baking sheet. Bake for 18-20 minutes or until golden brown. After taking from oven, brush top with melted butter if desired. Makes 6 to 8 servings.

BUTTER AND SOUR CREAM BISCUITS

2 (8 ounce) sticks butter, melted
1 cup sour cream
2 cups self-rising flour

Preheat oven to 400 degrees. In a large bowl, combine butter, sour cream, and flour. Mix well. Using mini-muffin pans, pour mixture to within ¼ inch of the top of each container. Bake for 15 minutes or until golden brown. Makes 10 to 12 servings.

Grief can take care of itself, but to get the full value of joy you must have somebody to divide it with.

Mark Twain

CHEDDAR CHEESE BISCUITS

2 cups Bisquick®
1½ cups milk
¾ cup grated sharp Cheddar cheese
¼ cup butter, melted
¼ teaspoon garlic powder

Preheat oven to 450 degrees. In a large bowl, combine Bisquick®, milk, and cheese. Mix well. Drop dough by spoonfuls onto ungreased baking sheet. Bake for 15 minutes or until lightly brown. In a small bowl, combine butter and garlic powder. Mix well. Lightly pour over each biscuit. Makes 6 to 8 servings.

*Lord,
help me
remember
today —
all you
taught me
yesterday.*

BLUE CHEESE BITES

10 refrigerated biscuits
¼ cup butter
3 tablespoons crumbled blue cheese

Preheat oven to 400 degrees. Quarter biscuits. In a 9 inch round baking pan, place biscuit quarters. In a small saucepan, melt butter and cheese. Drizzle mixture over top of biscuits. Bake until brown, 12 to 15 minutes. Makes 6 to 8 servings.

PARMESAN CHEESE BISCUITS

1 (9½ ounce) can biscuits
½ cup melted butter
½ cup Parmesan cheese

Dip biscuits in butter and sprinkle with cheese. Bake according to directions on biscuit package.

ROSEMARY BISCUITS

2 cups all-purpose flour, sifted
1 teaspoon salt
3 teaspoons baking powder
⅓ cup sugar
6 tablespoons margarine
½ cup milk
¼ cup fresh rosemary leaves, finely chopped

Preheat oven to 425 degrees. In a large bowl, combine flour, salt, baking powder, and sugar. Cut margarine into mixture. Add milk. Mix until stiff. Add rosemary leaves. Mix well. Roll to desired thickness and cut with small biscuit cutter. Place about 2 inches apart onto greased baking sheet. Bake for 15 minutes or until golden brown. Makes 6 to 8 servings.

WHIPPED CREAM BISCUITS

2 cups self-rising flour
1 cup whipping cream
2 tablespoons self-rising flour

Preheat oven to 400 degrees. In a large bowl, combine all ingredients. Mix well until a dough forms. Flour a surface, turn out dough on surface and knead briefly. Hand shape dough into small biscuits. Place biscuits onto greased baking sheet. Bake for 15 minutes or until golden brown. Makes 4 to 6 servings.

It is more important to discern the root problem than to become involved in discussing the twig on a branch.

Paul Little

HOMEMADE ROLLS

1 teaspoon salt
2 cups milk
½ cup sugar
½ cup margarine
2 (¼ ounce) packages yeast
6 cups all-purpose flour

Preheat oven to 350 degrees. In a medium saucepan, combine salt, milk, sugar, and margarine. Heat, but do not boil. Cool to lukewarm. Add yeast and let sit for 5 minutes. Stir to dissolve. Slowly add flour. Turn onto lightly floured board and knead slightly. Place in large lightly oiled bowl and let rise till doubled in size. Punch down and shape into rolls. Place rolls onto lightly greased baking sheet. Cover with dry cloth while rising. Bake oven until golden brown. Makes 6 to 8 servings.

TLC ROLLS

2 cups warm water
1 stick butter, melted
½ cup sugar
2 (¼ ounce) packages yeast
6 cups all-purpose flour
1 teaspoon salt
Cooking spray

In a large bowl, combine water and butter. Add sugar and yeast. When mixture turns white, add flour and salt. Mix well. Turn onto a floured surface or place in bread machine. Knead until dough is consistent. Place into greased bowl, cover, let rise. When the dough rises double in bulk, mash down, place on floured board. Pinch off enough for a good size roll and pat to shape. Lightly coat baking sheet with cooking spray. Place rolls on baking sheet. In a 400 degree oven, bake for approximately 10 to 12 minutes. Makes 6 to 8 servings.

One of the most important relationships you will have in your life is the one you have with yourself. Learn to love yourself, so you can have genuine love for others.

CROSSED-UP DINNER ROLLS

2 cups self-rising flour
1 cup milk
½ cup mayonnaise

Preheat oven to 425 degrees. In a large bowl, combine all
ingredients. Mix well. Drop 1 tablespoon dough on a
floured board. Roll into ball. Place onto greased baking
sheet. With knife, cut criss-cross marks across the top of
ball. Bake for 10 minutes. Makes 8 to 12 servings.

EIGHT TO TEN MINUTE ROLLS

4 tablespoons mayonnaise
1 cup milk
¼ teaspoon salt
2 cups self-rising flour

Preheat oven to 350 degrees. In a large bowl, combine
mayonnaise, milk, and salt. Add flour. Mix well. Pour
mixture into greased muffin pan. Bake for 8 to 10 minutes
or until golden brown. Makes 8 servings.

CHEESY BROWN 'N SERVE ROLLS

¼ cup butter, softened
¼ cup mayonnaise
¼ cup Parmesan cheese
1 dozen brown and serve rolls

Preheat oven to 350 degrees. In a small bowl, combine
butter, mayonnaise, and cheese. Mix well. Place rolls onto
ungreased baking sheet. Brush tops with cheese mixture.
Bake for 15 minutes until golden brown. Makes 6 servings.

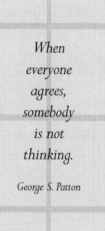

*When
everyone
agrees,
somebody
is not
thinking.*

George S. Patton

BUTTERMILK ROLLS

1 (¼ ounce) package yeast
1 cup warm water
½ cup sugar
½ cup vegetable oil
2 cups buttermilk
¼ teaspoon soda
1 teaspoon salt
4 teaspoons baking powder
6½ cups all-purpose flour

Preheat oven to 350 degrees. In a large bowl, dissolve yeast in water. Add sugar, oil, buttermilk, soda, salt, baking powder, and flour. Mix well. Chill. Pinch off small balls. Place balls onto greased baking sheet. Bake for 15 minutes or until brown. Makes 8 to 10 servings.

YUMMY STICKY ROLLS

3 tablespoons margarine
⅓ cup packed brown sugar
¾ cup granola-type cereal
1 (10 count) can butterflake refrigerated biscuits
Corn syrup

Preheat oven to 450 degrees. In a 9 inch round cake pan, melt margarine. Sprinkle brown sugar over margarine. Sprinkle cereal over mixture. Place biscuits in mixture. Turn biscuit over and place on baking sheet with space between each one. Sprinkle with more cereal and drizzle with syrup. Bake for 12 minutes. Makes 4-6 servings.

Indifference can be changed with patient persistence, and gentle speech can break down rigid defenses.

UPSIDE DOWN CARAMEL ROLLS

1 (4 servings) box cook and serve butterscotch pudding
1 cup chopped walnuts or pecans
24 frozen bread dough balls
½ cup butter
½ cup packed brown sugar

In a large bowl, combine dry pudding and nuts. Sprinkle nut mixture into 9x13 inch greased baking pan. Arrange bread dough balls in pan. In a small saucepan, melt butter and sugar. Mix well. Pour over bread rolls. Cover lightly with towel. Set out at room temperature 6 to 8 hours or overnight. In a 400 degree oven, bake for 20 minutes. Turn over on serving dish. Makes 12 servings.

BUSY DAY CINNAMON ROLLS

2 loaves frozen bread dough
½ cup margarine, melted
1 cup packed brown sugar
1 (4 serving) box instant vanilla instant pudding
2 tablespoons milk
1½ teaspoons cinnamon

Thaw bread dough. Do not let rise. Break one loaf in pieces. Arrange pieces in a 9x13 inch baking pan. In a large bowl, combine margarine, sugar, pudding mix, milk, and cinnamon. Stir until smooth. Pour mixture over dough in pan. Break other loaf into pieces and put on top. Let rise for 2 to 3 hours. In a 350 degree oven, bake for 25 to 30 minutes. Add glaze. Makes 8 to 12 servings.

GLAZE
2 tablespoons margarine
1 tablespoon orange juice
1 cup confectioners' sugar

In a medium bowl, combine all ingredients. Mix well. Pour over rolls.

*Like the rose
in which roses
have once been
distilled you
may break;
you may shatter
the vase if
you will,
but the scent
of the roses will
cling to it still.*

Anonymous

CINNAMON RAISIN COFFEE ROLLS

1 cup raisins
1 cup packed brown sugar
2 (8 count) cans refrigerated biscuits
½ cup butter, melted

Preheat oven to 350 degrees. In a medium bowl, combine raisins and sugar. Dip each biscuit in butter and then roll in sugar and raisin mixture. Place on baking sheet. Bake for 20 minutes. Makes 8 to 10 servings.

NUTTY CINNAMON RING

½ cup margarine
6 tablespoons packed light brown sugar
1¼ cups sifted confectioners' sugar, divided
1 teaspoon cinnamon
3 (9½ ounce) cans biscuits
½ cup chopped pecans
Cherries (optional)

Preheat oven to 350 degrees. In a small pan, melt margarine. In a medium bowl, combine brown sugar, ¾ cup confectioners' sugar, and cinnamon. Dip each biscuit in margarine, coat with sugar mixture. Place into greased 10 inch tube pan, overlapping edges. Sprinkle with pecans. Bake for 40 to 45 minutes. Remove cake from pan. In a small bowl, mix ½ cup confectioners' sugar with a few drops of water, and drizzle over cinnamon ring. Garnish with cherries, if desired. Makes 10 to 12 servings.

Life is not defined by what material things you have; its defined in the hearts of people you have come to know and love you.

Almost **Heaven**

PIES

CAKES

COOKIES

DESSERTS

CANDY

Wrapping It Up

1 King of Kings

Countless angels

1 cup reward

2 large golden streets

1 cup judgment

1 gallon forgiveness

48 cups friends

6 cups peace

Bottomless measure of praise

Forever singing

Covered with grace

MIRACLE PIE

1 cup Jeremiah 6:20 (sugar)
¼ cup Genesis 18:8 (butter)
4 Deuteronomy 22:6 (eggs)
½ cup II Kings 7:18 (all-purpose flour)
2 cups Hebrews 5:13 (milk)
1 cup Genesis 43:11 (flaked coconut)
¼ teaspoon Matthew 5:13 (salt)
½ teaspoon II Kings 23:15 (baking powder)
1 teaspoon vanilla

Preheat oven to 350 degrees. In a blender, combine all ingredients. Mix well. Pour into greased and floured 10 inch pie plate. Bake for 60 minutes. A crust will form on the bottom, pie filling in the center, and a coconut topping. Makes 6 to 8 servings.

GRANDMA'S PECAN PIE

¾ cup packed brown sugar
1 tablespoon butter
1 cup corn syrup
3 eggs, well beaten
1 teaspoon vanilla
1 cup coarsely, chopped pecans
⅛ teaspoon salt
1 (9 inch) unbaked pie shell

Preheat oven to 325 degrees. In a large bowl, combine all ingredients except pie shell. Mix well. Pour into unbaked pie shell. Bake 50 minutes or until pie is set. Makes 6 to 8 servings.

What if?
I don't know
if frogs had wings
they would not
bump their butts
so much.
But I do know
they have legs
and won't walk.

Martha Fulmer

STRAWBERRY PIE

¼ cup sugar
¼ teaspoon water
1 (8 ounce) package cream cheese
2 cups frozen whipped topping
1 (9 inch) graham cracker pie shell
3 cups halved fresh strawberries

In a large bowl, combine sugar, water, and cream cheese.
Stir until well blended. Fold in whipped topping. Spread
mixture into pie shell. Cover and chill 1 hour or until firm.
Arrange strawberries evenly over cream cheese mixture
just before serving. Makes 6 to 8 servings.

TROPICAL DELIGHT PIE

1 pint milk
½ cup sugar
3 tablespoons flour
1 tablespoon butter, melted
3 egg yolks, beaten
⅛ teaspoon salt
½ cup flaked coconut
1 teaspoon vanilla
1 (9 inch) baked pie shell
3 egg whites
6 tablespoons sugar

Preheat oven 350 degrees. In a large saucepan, heat milk,
sugar, flour, and butter. Add beaten egg yolks and salt.
Cook until thick. Add coconut and vanilla. Pour ingredients
into pie shell. In a small bowl, beat egg whites and sugar
until stiff. Spread egg white over pie. Sprinkle with additional coconut. Bake until top is lightly browned. Makes 6
to 8 servings.

*Recall it as often
as you wish,
a happy memory
never wears out.*

Libbie Fudim

OLD FASHIONED PUMPKIN PIE

3 eggs
3 cups pumpkin
1½ cups packed brown sugar
2 teaspoons cinnamon
1½ teaspoons ginger
¼ teaspoon salt
1 (9 inch) unbaked pie shell

Preheat oven to 350 degrees. In a large bowl, beat eggs until frothy. Add pumpkin, sugar, cinnamon, ginger, and salt. Mix well. Pour mixture into pie shell. Bake for 35 to 40 minutes or until done. Makes 6 to 8 servings.

ALMOST IMPOSSIBLE PIE

1¾ cups sugar
½ cup self-rising flour
4 eggs
½ stick butter, melted
2 teaspoons vanilla
2 cups milk
1 cup flaked coconut
½ teaspoon salt

Preheat oven to 350 degrees. In a blender, combine all ingredients. Mix well. Pour mixture into 9 inch greased pie plate. Bake for 40 minutes. Makes 6 to 8 servings.

*If I can stop
one heart
from breaking,
I shall not live in vain:
If I can ease one life
the aching,
or cool one pain,
or help one
fainting robin
unto his nest again,
I shall not live
in vain.*

Emily Dickinson

ICE BOX PINEAPPLE PIE

1 (14 ounce) can sweetened condensed milk
2 tablespoons lemon juice
1 (16 ounce) tub whipped topping
1 (16 ounce) can crushed pineapple
1 cup finely chopped pecans
1 (9 inch) graham cracker pie shell

In a large bowl, combine all ingredients. Mix well. Pour
mixture into pie shell. Chill for several hours. Makes 6
to 8 servings.

ICE BOX LEMON PIE

1 (9 ounce) tub whipped topping
1 (6 ounce) can frozen lemonade
1 (14 ounce) can sweetened condensed milk
1 (9 inch) graham cracker pie shell

In a large bowl, combine all ingredients. Mix well. Pour
mixture into pie shell. Chill for several hours. Makes 6
to 8 servings.

ICE CREAM LEMON PIE

1 (6 ounce) can frozen lemonade
1 pint vanilla ice cream, softened
3½ cups whipped topping
1 (9 inch) graham cracker pie shell
Yellow food coloring, optional

In a large bowl, combine lemonade and ice cream. Blend
in whipped topping. Add a few drops of food coloring, if
desired. Pour mixture into pie shell. Freeze until firm, at
least 4 hours. Makes 6 to 8 servings.

*When your
children have
children
they learn
to appreciate you.*

ICE CREAM FUDGE PIE

2 cups chocolate chips
1 cup marshmallow creme
1½ cups evaporated milk
1 (12 ounce) box vanilla wafers
½ gallon vanilla ice cream
1 cup fudge sauce
½ cup chopped walnuts

In a double boiler over low heat, melt chocolate chips, marshmallow creme, and milk together. Line bottom and side of a 9 inch pie pan with whole vanilla wafers to make the crust. Layer vanilla ice cream on crust, then fudge sauce, then ice cream, then more fudge sauce until the pie pan is full. Top with walnuts. Freeze. Makes 6 to 8 servings.

ROCKY ROAD PUDDING PIE

1 (4 serving) box instant chocolate pudding
½ cup miniature chocolate chips
½ cup miniature marshmallows
2¾ cups milk
1 (9 inch) graham cracker pie shell
1 (8 ounce) tub whipped topping
½ cup finely chopped pecans
Pecans
Chocolate chips

In a large bowl, combine pudding mix, chocolate chips, marshmallows, and milk. Pour mixture into pie shell. Place plastic wrap over filling to seal and prevent rubbery top. Refrigerate until serving time. Remove plastic wrap. Spread with whipped topping. Garnish with pecans and chocolate chips. Makes 6 to 8 servings.

All it took to tempt a man was a woman; it took the devil himself to tempt a woman.

Joe's Peanut Butter Pie

1½ cups creamy peanut butter
1 cup confectioners' sugar
1 tablespoon vanilla extract
1 (8 ounce) tub whipped topping
2 chocolate cookie pie crusts
½ gallon vanilla ice cream

In a large bowl, combine peanut butter, sugar, and vanilla. Mix well. Blend in whipped topping. Mix until smooth. Divide mixture equally between 2 pie shells. Spread evenly. Freeze for 30 to 45 minutes until solid. Remove ice cream from freezer and let soften for about 20 minutes. Place ice cream in a large bowl and stir until soft. Remove pies from freezer and add softened ice cream to both pies. Spread and smooth. Freeze for at least 1 hour, but overnight is best. Store the leftovers in the freezer. Makes 6 to 8 servings.

Nutty Chocolate Pie

¼ pound butter
1 square unsweetened chocolate
1 cup sugar
2 eggs
½ cup self-rising flour
½ cup chopped nuts, optional

Preheat oven at 325 degrees. In a large saucepan, melt butter and chocolate over low heat. Cool slightly. By hand beat in sugar and eggs. Stir in flour. Add nuts. Pour into greased pie pan. Bake for 35 to 40 minutes. Makes 6 to 8 servings.

Worry doesn't take the sorrow out of today; it only takes the strength out of tomorrow.

SCRIPTURE CAKE

1 cup Judges 5:25 (butter)
2 cups Jeremiah 6:20 (sugar)
6 Jeremiah 17:11 (eggs)
4½ cups I Kings 4:22 (all-purpose flour)
2 teaspoons Amos 4:5 (baking powder)
½ cup Judges 4:19 (milk)
2 teaspoons I Samuel 14:25 (honey)
½ cup I Kings 4:22 (all-purpose flour)
2 cups I Samuel 30:12 (raisins)
2 cups Nahum 3:12 (figs)
Season to taste with II Chronicles 9:9 (spices)

Preheat oven to 350 degrees. In a large bowl, cream butter and slowly add sugar. Blend in well-beaten egg yolks. Sift flour and baking powder. Add milk and honey mixture to dry ingredients. Beat well. Coat raisins and figs with flour. Add to batter. Beat egg whites until stiff and fold into batter. Pour mixture into greased tube pan. Bake for 1 hour and 15 minutes. Makes 10 to 12 servings.

To avoid forbidden fruit, stay out of the devil's orchard.

RASPBERRIES AND LEMON CAKE

1 box angel food cake mix
½ cup confectioners' sugar
1 teaspoon lemon juice
8 ounces raspberries
Whipped topping

Bake cake according to package directions. Cool and prick top with fork. In a medium bowl, combine sugar and lemon juice. Spread on cake. Spread whipped topping on cake. Sprinkle with raspberries. Makes 10 to 12 servings.

EVE'S APPLE CAKE

3 eggs
1½ cups vegetable oil
2 cups sugar
3 cups all-purpose flour
1 teaspoon salt
1 teaspoon baking soda
2 teaspoons vanilla
3 cups chopped apples
1½ cups chopped nuts

Preheat oven to 350 degrees. In a large bowl, combine all
ingredients. Mix well. Pour ingredients into 2 greased 9
inch round cake pans until each pan is half full. Bake for
one hour. Makes 10 to 12 servings.

TOPPING
1 stick margarine or butter
¼ cup milk
1 cup packed light brown sugar

Remove cake from oven and place layers on a cake plate.
In a medium saucepan, combine butter, milk, and sugar.
Place on stove and bring to a boil. Boil for 2 or 3 minutes.
Cool and spread on cake.

APPLE CREAM CAKE

1 box yellow cake mix
1 (15 ounce) can apple pie filling
1 (8 ounce) package cream cheese, softened
½ cup oil
4 eggs

Preheat oven to 350 degrees. In a large bowl, combine all
ingredients. Pour mixture into greased and floured bundt
pan. Bake for 60 minutes. Makes 10 to 12 servings.

*The Bible
is meant
to be bread
for our
daily use,
not cake
for a special
occasion.*

POP CAKE

1 (12 ounce) can strawberry pop
1 (6 ounce) package of strawberry flavored gelatin
1 box yellow cake mix
1 (4 serving) box instant vanilla pudding
4 ounces whipped topping

In a large saucepan, bring pop to a boil and stir in gelatin. Chill, not to jelly form. Bake cake according to package instructions. Remove cake from oven. Pierce top of cake with a fork. Pour gelatin mixture over cake and chill for 30 minutes. Prepare instant pudding according to package instructions. Spread over cake. Spread whipped topping over pudding. Makes 10 to 12 servings.

FRENCH CHERRY VANILLA CAKE

1 stick margarine
1 box French vanilla cake mix, dry
2 eggs
1 (20 ounce) can cherry pie filling
2 cups chopped pecans

Preheat oven to 350 degrees. In a large bowl, combine all ingredients. Pour mixture into greased and floured bundt or tube pan. Bake for one hour. Makes 10 to 12 servings.

CHERRY CREAM CAKE

1 box yellow cake mix
1 (15 ounce) can cherry pie filling
1 (8 ounce) package cream cheese, softened
½ cup oil
4 eggs

Preheat oven to 350 degrees. In a large bowl, combine all ingredients. Pour mixture into greased and floured bundt pan. Bake for 60 minutes. Makes 10 to 12 servings.

Kind words can be short and easy to speak, but their echoes are truly endless.

Mother Teresa

BLUEBERRY CREAM CAKE

1 box yellow cake mix
1 (15 ounce) can whole blueberries, drained
1 (8 ounce) package cream cheese, softened
½ cup oil
4 eggs

Preheat oven to 350 degrees. In a large bowl, combine all
ingredients. Pour mixture into greased and floured bundt
pan. Bake for 60 minutes. Makes 10 to 12 servings.

BUTTER PECAN FRUIT CAKE

1 (15½ ounce) can fruit cocktail, undrained
1 box butter pecan cake mix
1½ sticks margarine, melted

Preheat oven to 350 degrees. Pour fruit cocktail into an
9x13 inch baking pan. Sprinkle cake mix over fruit. Pour
margarine over cake mix. Mix well. Bake for 45 minutes.
Makes 10 to 12 servings.

Swallowing
your pride
will never give
you indigestion.

STARS AND STRIPES CAKE

2 loaves sponge cake, sliced
1 (8 ounce) tub whipped topping, thawed
2 cups blueberries, divided
4 cups sliced strawberries, thick, divided

Line the bottom of an 9x13 inch baking pan with cake
slices. Cover with whipped topping, strawberries, and
blueberries. Cover with more slices of sponge cake. Frost
with whipped topping. In left corner, place blueberries in
a rectangular shape to form stars. Place strawberries in
straight line across to form stripes. Finished product will
look like a flag. Makes 10 to 12 servings.

CHERRY PINEAPPLE DUMP CAKE

1 (16 ounce) can crushed pineapple, undrained
1 (21 ounce) can cherry pie filling, undrained
1 box yellow or white cake mix
1½ cups chopped walnuts (optional)
2 sticks butter
Whipped topping

Preheat oven to 325 degrees. Pour crushed pineapple in a 9x13 inch baking pan. Spread cherry pie filling over pineapple. Sprinkle dry cake mix over fruit, sprinkle nuts, and dice butter and dot top. Bake for 1 hour. Top with whipped topping, if desired. Makes 10 to 12 servings.

CREAM CHEESE ANGEL CAKE

1 (8 ounce) package cream cheese, softened
1 cup confectioners' sugar
1 (8 ounce) tub whipped topping, thawed
1 (14 ounce) angel food cake
2 (21 ounce) cans blueberry pie filling

In a large mixing bowl, beat cream cheese and sugar. Fold in whipped topping. Tear cake into small 1 or 2 inch cubes and place into a 9x13 inch dish. Add cheese mixture and spread evenly. Top with pie filling. Cover and chill for at least 3 hours before cutting into squares to serve. Makes 10 to 12 servings.

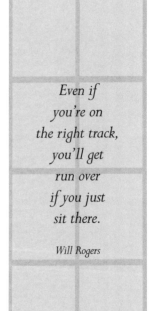

Even if you're on the right track, you'll get run over if you just sit there.

Will Rogers

CHOCOLATE ANGEL CAKE

8 ounces milk chocolate
1 (16 ounce) tub whipped topping
1 cup chopped almonds
1 large angel food cake

In a double boiler, over hot water, melt chocolate. Cool. In a large bowl, fold whipped topping and almonds into chocolate. Split cake in half. Spread chocolate mixture between layers. Frost cake with remaining mixture. Store in refrigerator. Makes 10 to 12 servings.

LOTS OF COCONUT CAKE

1 box white cake mix
3 eggs
¼ cup oil
1 (4 ounce) can flaked coconut
1 cup sour cream
1 (14 ounce) can cream of coconut
1 (4 ounce) can flaked coconut
1 (8 ounce) tub whipped topping

Preheat oven to 350 degrees. In a large bowl, combine cake mix, eggs, oil, coconut, and sour cream. Beat at low speed with electric mixer until blended. Beat at high speed for 2 minutes. Pour into greased 9x13 inch baking pan. Bake for 20 minutes or until done. Pierce cake with fork. Pour cream of coconut over hot cake. Cool in pan. In a large bowl, combine remaining can of coconut and whipped topping. Mix well. Spread over cool cake. Cover with plastic wrap. Chill in refrigerator overnight. Makes 10 to 12 servings.

People may doubt what you say, but they will always believe what you do.

JUDY'S RAVING ITALIAN CREAM CAKE

½ cup butter
½ cup vegetable shortening
2 cups sugar
5 large eggs, separated
1 tablespoon vanilla extract
2 cups all-purpose flour
1 teaspoon baking soda
1 cup buttermilk
1 cup flaked coconut
Toasted pecan halves
Chopped pecan halves

Preheat oven to 350 degrees. In a large bowl using an electric mixer, beat butter and shortening at medium speed until fluffy. Gradually add sugar. Mix well. Add egg yolks, one at a time, beating until blended after each addiction. Add vanilla, continue beating. In a bowl, combine flour and soda. Add to butter mixture alternately with buttermilk, beginning and ending with flour mixture. Beat on low speed until blended after each addition. Stir in coconut. Pour egg whites in a small bowl, beat with mixer, on high until stiff peaks form. Fold egg whites into batter. Pour batter into three 9 inch round floured cake pans. Bake for 25 minutes or until a wooden toothpick inserted in the middle comes out clean. Remove from pans. Cool on wire racks. Top with icing and garnish with whole and chopped pecans.

FROSTING
1 cup chopped pecans
1 (8 ounce) package cream cheese, softened
½ cup butter, softened
1 tablespoon vanilla extract
1 (16 ounce) box confectioners' sugar, sifted

Preheat oven to 350 degrees. Using a shallow baking pan, bake pecans for 5 to 10 minutes or until toasted. Cool. In a large bowl, combine cream cheese, butter, and vanilla. Using an electric mixer, beat on medium speed until creamy. Add confectioners' sugar, beat on low speed until blended. Beat on high speed until smooth. Add pecans. Makes 10 to 12 servings.

The Lord's goodness surrounds us at every moment. I walk through it almost with difficulty, as through thick grass and flowers.

R.W. Barbour

OH NO POUND CAKE

1 cup butter
½ cup vegetable shortening
3 cups sugar
5 large eggs
3½ cups all-purpose flour
4 tablespoons cocoa
½ teaspoon salt
1 cup milk
2 teaspoons vanilla

Preheat oven to 325 degrees. In a large bowl, cream butter, shortening, and sugar. Add eggs. Mix well. In a separate bowl, combine flour, cocoa, and salt. Add to sugar mixture. Blend in milk and vanilla. Pour mixture into greased and floured tube pan. Bake for 1 hour and 25 minutes. Cool in pan. Makes 10 to 12 servings.

FAST AND FANCY POUND CAKE

1 (4 serving) box cook and serve vanilla pudding
2½ cups milk
1 (16 ounce) pound cake
1 (8 ounce) jar apricot jam
1 (16 ounce) tub whipped topping
1 cup flaked coconut

In a large bowl, prepare pudding according to box directions using 2½ cups milk. Split cake into 4 layers. Spread jam and pudding between layers. Frost cake with whipped topping. Sprinkle with coconut. Refrigerate until serving time. Makes 10 to 12 servings.

Just about the time a woman thinks her work is done, she becomes a grandmother.

Edward H. Dreschnack

CHOCOLATE CHEESECAKE BALLS

3 (8 ounce) packages cream cheese
1½ cups miniature chocolate chips
1 cup confectioners' sugar, sifted
1¼ cups pecans, chopped
1 (7 ounce) milk chocolate candy bar, shaved
Ginger snaps

In a large bowl, combine cream cheese, chips, and sugar.
Mix well. Shape into small balls. Chill before serving. Place
on serving plate, cover with chopped pecans, and garnish
with chocolate shavings. Serve with ginger snaps. Makes 16
to 18 servings.

PINEAPPLE AND CREAM CHEESE CAKE

1 teaspoon margarine
1 (8¼ ounce) can crushed pineapple, with juice
2 cups all-purpose flour
2 teaspoons soda
2 eggs
1 cup chopped walnuts or pecans

Preheat oven to 350 degrees. Coat a 9x13 inch baking pan
with margarine. In a large bowl, combine pineapple, flour,
soda, eggs, and nuts. Mix well. Pour mixture into pan. Bake
for 45 minutes for a metal pan or 35 minutes for a glass
pan. Makes 10 to 12 servings.

FROSTING
2 cups confectioners' sugar
1 (8 ounce) package cream cheese, softened
1 stick melted butter

In a large bowl, combine sugar, cream cheese, and melted
butter. Spread mixture on cake. Cake may remain in the
pan for serving.

When things
are going badly,
take time to count
your blessings.
'For who knoweth
what is good
for man in
this life.'

Ecclesiastes 6:12a

CLOUDS IN CHOCOLATE

1 cup all-purpose flour
¼ cup unsweetened cocoa powder
1 teaspoon baking soda
¼ teaspoon salt
½ cup sugar
¼ cup solid vegetable shortening
1 egg white
½ cup low-fat (1%) milk
¾ cup marshmallow creme

Preheat oven to 425 degrees. In a medium bowl, combine flour, cocoa, baking soda, and salt. In a medium bowl, use an electric mixer on medium speed, beat sugar, shortening, and egg white until fluffy. Stir in flour mixture, then milk, until just blended. Drop dough by spoonfuls onto large, ungreased baking sheet. Bake until top springs back when lightly touched, 5-7 minutes. Cool completely on baking sheet. Spoon 2 teaspoons marshmallow creme on half the cookies. Top with the remaining cookies. Can be stored in an airtight container for up to 3 days. Makes 12 to 14 servings.

AFTER SCHOOL BUTTER COOKIES

1 stick butter, softened
2 cups self-rising flour
½ cup sugar
1 cup walnuts or pecans, halves

Preheat oven to 350 degrees. In a large bowl, combine all ingredients. Mix well. Roll on floured board. Make small balls. Place onto ungreased baking sheet. Place 1 walnut or pecan half the middle of each cookie. Bake for 10 to 12 minutes. Also good without the nuts. Makes 8 to 10 servings.

Let your public self be true to who you are. You have to live with yourself in both places.

COOKIE JAR SUGAR COOKIES

2 cups butter
2 cups sugar
4 egg yolks
4 cups self-rising flour

Preheat oven to 375 degrees. In a large mixing bowl, cream butter and sugar. Add egg yolks and flour. Mix well. Drop mixture by teaspoonfuls onto ungreased baking sheet. Sprinkle with favorite sugar decorations. Bake for 8 to 10 minutes. Makes 10 to 12 servings.

ROCKY TRAIL BAR COOKIES

1 (18 ounce) package refrigerated
   sugar cookie dough, softened
1 (6 ounce) bag nut and chocolate trail mix

Preheat oven to 350 degrees. In a large bowl, combine cookie dough and trail mix. Mix well. Spread mixture evenly into ungreased 8 inch square baking pan. Baked for 30 minutes. Let stand 5 minutes. Cut into 8 bars. Makes 8 servings.

COCONUT MACAROONS

2 ounces chocolate
½ pound shredded coconut
1 (14 ounce) can sweetened condensed milk
1 cup finely chopped nuts
½ cup self-rising flour

In a double boiler, melt chocolate. Add coconut, milk, nuts, and flour. Drop mixture by spoonfuls onto greased baking sheet. Bake for 20 minutes. Makes 10 to 12 servings.

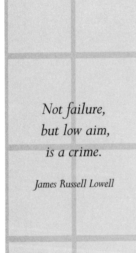

*Not failure,
but low aim,
is a crime.*

James Russell Lowell

CHOCOLATE COOKIES

2 cups butter
1½ cups sugar
1½ cups packed brown sugar
4 eggs
2 teaspoons vanilla
4 cups self-rising flour
2 teaspoons salt
2 teaspoons soda
12 ounces chocolate chips

Preheat oven to 350 degrees. In a large bowl, combine butter, sugars, eggs, and vanilla together. Add flour, salt, soda, and chocolate chips. Mix well. Drop mixture by teaspoonfuls onto ungreased baking sheet. Bake 8 to 10 minutes for desired crispness. Makes 10 to 12 servings.

NO BAKE COOKIES

2 cups sugar
½ cup margarine
½ cup milk
3 tablespoons cocoa
⅛ teaspoon salt
⅓ cup peanut butter
½ cup flaked coconut
3 cups quick oatmeal
1 teaspoon vanilla

In a large saucepan, combine sugar, margarine, milk, cocoa, and salt. Boil for one minute. Add peanut butter, coconut, oatmeal, and vanilla until thoroughly coated. Drop mixture by tablespoonfuls onto waxed paper and let cool. Makes 12 to 14 servings.

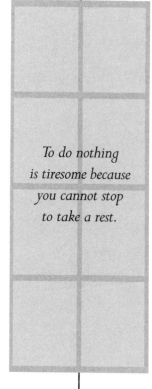

*To do nothing
is tiresome because
you cannot stop
to take a rest.*

PEANUT BUTTER COOKIES

1 cup shortening (butter flavor)
1 cup peanut butter
1 cup packed brown sugar
1 cup sugar
2 eggs
1 teaspoon vanilla
2¼ cups all-purpose flour
2 teaspoons baking soda
¼ teaspoon salt

Preheat oven to 350 degrees. In a large bowl, combine shortening and peanut butter. Add sugars and mix well. Add eggs, vanilla, flour, baking soda, and salt. Mix well. Drop mixture by teaspoonfuls onto ungreased baking sheet. Bake for 10 to 12 minutes. Makes 10 to 12 servings.

CRUNCHY PEANUT COOKIES

1 box yellow cake mix
2 eggs
2 tablespoons water
½ cup vegetable oil
1 cup crunchy peanut butter
¼ cup peanuts, skins removed

Preheat oven to 350 degrees. In a large bowl, combine all ingredients. Drop mixture by teaspoonfuls onto ungreased baking sheet. Bake for 8 to 10 minutes. Makes 10 to 12 servings.

Worry is like a rocking chair — it will keep you rocking but will never get you anywhere. A lot of motion burning up a lot of energy.

TINY GINGER SNAPS

¾ cup solid vegetable shortening
1 cup sugar
1 egg
¼ cup molasses
2 cups flour
1½ teaspoons soda
1 teaspoon ground cloves
1 teaspoon ginger
½ cup sugar

Preheat oven to 350 degrees. In a large bowl, cream
shortening and sugar. Add egg and molasses. Beat until
smooth. In a separate bowl, sift flour, soda, cloves, ginger,
and sugar. Add to creamed mixture. Beat until smooth.
Make into teaspoon-size balls. Roll in sugar. Place balls
onto ungreased baking sheet. Bake for 8 to 10 minutes.
Makes 24 to 26 servings.

COOKIE BRITTLE

2 cups softened butter
1 cup sugar
2 teaspoons vanilla
4 cups self-rising flour
1 teaspoon salt
12 ounces chocolate chips
2 cups chopped pecans

Preheat oven to 350 degrees. In a large bowl, combine all
ingredients. Mix well. Press mixture into 9x13 inch ungreased baking pan. Sprinkle with nuts. Bake for 20 minutes.
Cool and cut into squares. Makes 10 to 12 servings.

*God gives
food to every
living thing,
for His
loving kindness
continues forever.
It makes
no difference
what we do.
He still
loves us.*

FORGOTTEN COOKIES

2 eggs whites
¾ cup sugar
½ cup nuts
6 ounces chocolate chips

Preheat oven to 375 degrees. In a large bowl, beat egg whites with electric mixer until soft peaks form. Fold in sugar and continue to beat until very stiff. Fold in nuts and chocolate chips. Drop mixture by tablespoonfuls onto greased baking sheet. Place in hot oven. Turn off heat to the oven. Leave overnight or until oven is room temperature. Makes 10-12 servings.

CATHEDRAL COOKIES

1 (12 ounce) package chocolate chips
4 tablespoons margarine
2 eggs
1 cup chopped nuts
1 (10.5 ounce) package miniature marshmallows
1 cup confectioners' sugar

In a large saucepan, melt chocolate chips and margarine. Remove from heat. In a large bowl, beat eggs. Gradually add chocolate mixture, nuts, and marshmallows. Form into long roll. Roll in confectioners' sugar. Refrigerate. Slice and serve. Makes 8 to 10 servings.

Sometimes we just have to do the hard stuff. We can get strength from the Lord if we just ask.

BAPTIST CHEWS

1 (16 ounce) box brown sugar
4 eggs, beaten
2 cups all-purpose flour
1 teaspoon vanilla
1 cup chopped nuts
½ cup flaked coconut

Preheat oven to 350 degrees. In a large bowl, combine sugar, eggs, and flour. Add vanilla, nuts, and coconut. Pour ingredients into 12x18 inch floured baking pan. Bake for 15 minutes. Makes 10 to 12 servings.

ICING
1 (16 ounce) box confectioners' sugar
½ cup margarine
¼ cup milk

In a medium bowl, cream sugar and margarine. Add milk. Mix well. Spread mixture on top of chews. Cut to preferred sizes.

CHOCOLATE PEANUT BUTTER SQUARES

1 pound confectioners' sugar
1 cup crunchy peanut butter
1 cup butter
1¼ cup graham cracker crumbs
6 ounces chocolate chips

In a large bowl, combine sugar, peanut butter, butter, and graham cracker crumbs. Press mixture into 9x13 inch pan. In a small saucepan, melt chocolate chips. Spread chocolate over top of mixture. Refrigerate. Makes 12 to 14 servings.

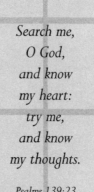

Search me,
O God,
and know
my heart:
try me,
and know
my thoughts.

Psalms 139:23

Almost Heaven

SUPER COOKIES

2 cups butter, softened
2 cups sugar
2 cups packed brown sugar
3 cups oats
4 cups all-purpose flour
1 teaspoon salt
2 teaspoons baking powder
2 teaspoons soda
24 ounces semisweet chocolate chips
2 cups chopped pecans

Preheat oven to 375 degrees. In a large mixing bowl, cream butter and sugars until light and fluffy. In a blender, process oats and flour a small amount at a time until pulverized. Add salt, baking powder, and soda to oat mixture. Mix well. Add chocolate chips and pecans. Shape into golf ball-sized cookies. Place cookies 2 inches apart onto ungreased baking sheet. Bake for 6 minutes. Cool on wire rack. Makes 12 to 14 servings.

SWEDISH BUTTER ALMOND COOKIES

1 cup butter
½ cup sugar
1 teaspoon almond extract
¼ teaspoon salt
2 cups self-rising flour
1 cup sugar

Preheat oven to 350 degrees. In a large bowl, cream butter and sugar. Add almond extract. Blend in salt and flour. Chill dough. Roll out into one-inch balls. Roll balls in sugar. Bake for 12 to 15 minutes. Makes 10 to 12 servings.

The heart is the best companion in work. Mother would say, 'You can do anything if your heart is in it.'

LOW FAT CHEWY FRUIT AND OATMEAL BARS

¾ cup packed brown sugar
½ cup sugar
8 ounces vanilla or plain low fat yogurt
2 egg whites, lightly beaten
2 tablespoons vegetable oil
2 tablespoons fat-free milk
2 teaspoons vanilla
1½ cups all-purpose flour
1 teaspoon baking soda
¼ teaspoon cinnamon
½ teaspoon salt
3 cups old-fashioned oatmeal
1 cup diced dried mixed fruit, raisins
   or dried cranberries

Preheat oven to 350 degrees. In a large bowl, combine sugars, yogurt, egg whites, oil, milk, and vanilla. Mix well. In medium bowl, combine flour, baking soda, cinnamon, salt, oatmeal, and dried fruit. Mix well. Spread dough into greased 9x13 inch baking pan. Bake 28 to 32 minutes or until golden brown. Cool and cut into bars. Makes 8 to 10 servings.

BERRY OATMEAL BARS

3 packages yellow cake mix
7½ cups oats
4½ sticks butter, melted
3 tablespoons water
36 ounces jam (berry, apricot, or strawberry)

Preheat oven to 375 degrees. In a large bowl, combine cake mix, oats, and butter. Stir until crumbly. Spread ½ of the mixture (approximately 9 cups) into 9x13 inch baking pan and press firmly. In a medium bowl, combine water and jam. Spread mixture evenly in pan. Cover with remaining crumb mixture. Pat firmly. Bake for 20 minutes. Top should be light brown. Cool completely. Makes 10 to 12 servings.

With each honor there comes an equal responsibility.

OATMEAL RAISIN CLASSICS

¾ cup solid vegetable shortening
1 cup packed brown sugar
½ cup sugar
¼ cup milk
1 egg
1 teaspoon vanilla
1 cup all-purpose flour
1 teaspoon cinnamon
½ teaspoon baking soda
¼ teaspoon salt
3 cups old-fashioned oatmeal
1 cup chopped pecans
1 cup raisins

Preheat oven to 350 degrees. In a large bowl, combine shortening, brown sugar, sugar, milk, egg, and vanilla. Mix until fluffy. Add flour, cinnamon, baking soda, and salt. Add oats, pecans, and raisins. Drop mixture by teaspoonfuls onto greased baking sheet. Bake in upper third of oven for 12 to 15 minutes. Makes 10 to 12 servings.

CHOCOLATE BUTTERSCOTCH DOLLIES

1½ cups graham cracker crumbs
6 ounces chocolate chips
6 ounces butterscotch chips
1 cup pecans, chopped
7 ounces flaked coconut
1 cup sweetened condensed milk
1 (8 ounce) stick butter, melted

Preheat oven to 350 degrees. Sprinkle cracker crumbs into greased 9x13 inch baking pan. Layer chocolate chips, butterscotch chips, pecans, and coconut. Pour milk and butter over top of layered ingredients. Bake for 25 to 30 minutes. Cool and cut into squares. Makes 10 to 12 servings.

Despite beautiful affirmation from others, we must believe in ourselves. Sometimes just believing in yourself as a child of God is our biggest challenge.

RUSSIAN TEA COOKIES

1 stick butter, softened
½ cup confectioners' sugar
1 teaspoon vanilla
½ teaspoon salt
2½ cups self-rising flour
¾ cup chopped walnuts
Confectioners' sugar (coating)

Preheat oven to 400 degrees. In a large bowl, cream butter, sugar, vanilla, and salt. Add flour and walnuts. Roll into tablespoon size balls. Bake for 10 minutes, roll into sugar while still warm. Makes 8 to 10 servings.

CHOCOLATE BROWNIES

1 stick margarine
1 (2 ounce) square unsweetened chocolate
1 cup sugar
2 eggs
⅔ cup all-purpose flour
½ teaspoon baking powder
½ teaspoon salt
1 teaspoon vanilla

Preheat oven to 350 degrees. In a medium saucepan, melt margarine and chocolate. Remove from heat. In a large bowl, combine margarine, chocolate, and sugar. Mix until smooth. Add eggs, one at a time. Mix well. Blend in flour, salt, and baking powder. Add vanilla. Mix until smooth. Pour mixture into greased 8x8 inch baking pan. Bake for 20 minutes or until a toothpick comes out clean. Cool completely. Cut and serve. Makes 8 to 10 servings.

When your work speaks for itself, don't interrupt.

Henry J. Kaiser

EASY HOT FUDGE SAUCE

3 tablespoons cocoa
1 cup sugar
1 (5 ounce) can evaporated milk
1 tablespoon butter
1 teaspoon vanilla

In a large saucepan, combine cocoa, sugar, and milk. Bring to a boil, stirring constantly. Remove from heat. Add butter and vanilla. Mix well. Makes 2 to 4 servings.

PEACH AND BLUEBERRY CRISP

3 cups fresh or thawed frozen sliced peaches, undrained
1 cup fresh or thawed frozen blueberries, undrained
2 tablespoons sugar
¼ teaspoon ground nutmeg
1 cup oats
2 tablespoons crisp rice cereal
2 tablespoons self-rising flour
1 tablespoon packed brown sugar
1 tablespoon butter
¼ teaspoon ground cinnamon

Preheat oven to 375 degrees. In an 8 inch round baking pan, combine peaches and blueberries. In a small bowl, combine sugar and nutmeg. Sprinkle over fruit. Toss gently. In a medium bowl, combine oats, rice cereal, flour, brown sugar, butter, and cinnamon. Sprinkle over fruit. Bake, uncovered, 35 to 40 minutes or until peaches are tender and topping is brown. Makes 8 to 10 servings.

*Most people
ask for happiness
on condition.
Happiness
can be felt
only if
you don't set
any conditions.*

Arthur Rubenstein

PEACHY VANILLA COBBLER

1 cup sugar
1 cup self-rising flour
1 egg
1 stick butter, melted
1 teaspoon vanilla
1 teaspoon cinnamon
1 (29 ounce) can peaches, undrained

Preheat oven to 350 degrees. In a medium bowl, combine sugar, flour, egg, butter, and vanilla. Pour peaches into greased 9x13 inch baking pan. Cut peaches into smaller pieces. Spoon flour mixture over peaches and stir. Bake for 20 minutes or until brown. Remove from oven. Makes 8 to 10 servings.

TOPPING

1 tablespoon butter, melted
2 tablespoons sugar
1 tablespoon cinnamon

Brush baked cobbler with melted butter. In a small bowl, combine cinnamon and sugar. Mix well. Sprinkle on top of cobbler.

It's the little things that we do for others that makes them smile on the inside.

BAKED VANILLA CUSTARD

3 cups milk
3 eggs
¾ cup sugar
¼ teaspoon salt
1 teaspoon vanilla
¼ teaspoon cinnamon

Preheat oven to 350 degrees. In a medium saucepan, scald milk. In a large bowl, beat eggs. Blend in sugar, salt, and vanilla. Slowly pour scalded milk into mixture. Pour mixture into a 2-quart baking dish and sprinkle with cinnamon. Bake, in a hot water bath for 45 minutes. Makes 4 to 6 servings.

PURE DELIGHT PUDDING

1 cup self-rising flour
1 stick butter, melted
½ cup chopped pecans
1 cup confectioners' sugar
1 cup whipped topping
1 (4 serving) box instant vanilla pudding
1 (4 serving) box instant chocolate pudding

Preheat oven to 350 degrees. In a large bowl, combine flour, butter, and nuts. Press mixture into greased 9x13 inch baking pan. Bake for 15 minutes. In a medium bowl, combine sugar and whipped topping. Spread over cooled crust. In a medium bowl, prepare pudding mixes according to package directions. Pour pudding over crust. Top with whipped topping. Chill. Makes 8 to 10 servings.

COCONUT CHOCOLATE BALLS

1 (12 ounce) package white chocolate baking chips
½ stick margarine
16 large marshmallows
2 cups quick cooking oats
1 cup flaked coconut

In a medium saucepan, melt chocolate chips, margarine, and marshmallows over low heat. Stir until smooth. Blend in oats and coconut. Mix well. Drop mixture by rounded teaspoonfuls onto waxed paper lined baking sheets. Chill until set. Store in airtight container. Makes 10 to 12 servings.

*My little
children,
let us not love
in word,
nether in tongue;
but in deed
and in truth.*

1 John 3:18

CHERRY CRISP

1 (21 ounce) can cherry pie filling
½ teaspoon almond extract
½ cup self-rising flour
½ cup packed brown sugar
1 teaspoon ground cinnamon
1 stick butter, softened
½ cup chopped walnuts
¼ cup flaked coconut
Ice cream or whipped cream (optional)

Preheat oven to 350 degrees. In an 8x8 inch baking pan, combine pie filling and almond extract. Set aside. In a medium bowl, combine flour, sugar, and cinnamon. Mix well. Blend in butter with a fork until mixture is crumbly. Add walnuts and coconut. Mix well. Sprinkle mixture over cherry pie filling. Bake 25 minutes or until golden brown on top and filling is bubbly. Serve warm or at room temperature. If desired top with ice cream or whipped cream. Makes 10 to 12 servings.

It is easier to fight for one's principles than to live up to them.

Alfred Adler

ICE CREAM FUDGE DESSERT

19 ice cream sandwiches
1 (12 ounce) carton whipped topping, thawed
1 (11¾ ounce) jar hot fudge ice cream topping
1 cup salted peanuts

In ungreased 9x13 inch baking pan, place one whole and one half sandwich along short side. Arrange eight sandwiches in opposite direction in the pan. Spread with half of the whipped topping. Spoon fudge topping by teaspoonfuls onto whipped topping. Sprinkle with ½ cup peanuts. Repeat layers with remaining ice cream sandwiches, whipped topping, and peanuts (pan will be full). Cover and freeze. Remove from freezer 20 minutes before serving. Makes 18 to 20 servings.

HEARTWARMING ICE CREAM BALLS

**1 gallon of any flavor ice cream, vanilla is great
1 cup flaked coconut
1 cup chocolate syrup
1 cup hot fudge
1 cup caramel**

Make balls out of ice cream about the size of a tennis ball. Roll each one in coconut, chocolate pieces, or nuts. Place in a container, cover and place in freezer. At serving time place chocolate syrup, hot fudge, or caramel in an ice cream dish. Place ice cream ball in the middle of the sauce and serve. Makes 8 to 10 servings.

WARM FRUIT SORBET

**1 cup raspberries or blueberries
4 tablespoons apple juice
6 tablespoons lemon sherbet (or vanilla ice cream)
Nuts**

In a small saucepan, heat berries and apple juice. On a serving plate, place lemon sherbet or vanilla ice cream in the center. Arrange warm berries on the side. Garnish with nuts if desired. Makes 2 servings.

FRESH FRUIT BOATS

Cut one fresh pineapple in quarters being careful not to remove green top. Gently remove core strip from each quarter. Use a sharp knife to scoop pineapple from shell. Cut into chunks. Combine chunks with fresh strawberries and blueberries. Fill each shell with mixed fruit and serve with a scoop of your choice of sherbet. Makes 8 to 10 servings.

Someone once said, 'It's hard to keep a good man down.' That's true unless he is down on his knees praying.

MELON BASKET

1 watermelon
1 good size cantaloupe
1 honeydew melon

Remove rind on bottom of watermelon so that it will
not rock when placed on a table. Remove top third of
watermelon, slowly and carefully, grooving and fluting
edges. Scoop out remaining melon, removing as many
seeds as possible. Cut melons into chunks. Fill empty
melon 'basket' with chunks of all three melons. Serve
cold or on a bed of ice. Can be served with a scoop of
sherbet on top. Makes 18 to 20 servings.

DOUBLE DIPPED CHOCOLATE COVERED STRAWBERRIES

1½ pound large, long stemmed strawberries
1 (8 ounce) semisweet chocolate bar, broken

Wash strawberries in cold water, dry and refrigerate for
3 hours. In a medium saucepan, melt broken chocolate
until smooth, stirring often. Holding strawberry by the
stem, dip into chocolate. Place on tray lined with wax
paper. Refrigerate until chocolate becomes firm. Makes
6 to 8 servings.

*Add to
your faith
virtue;
and to virtue
knowledge...
And to godliness
brotherly
kindness;
and to brotherly
kindness
charity.*

II Peter 1:5-7

DIVINE PINEAPPLE BANANA STRAWBERRIES

1 quart fresh strawberries, halved or quartered
1 (20 ounce) can pineapple chunks, well drained
2 bananas, sliced
1 (18 ounce) carton strawberry glaze

In a medium bowl, combine strawberries, pineapple chunks, and bananas. Fold in the strawberry glaze and chill. This is wonderful served over pound cake or in sherbet glasses. Makes 2 to 4 servings.

WARM BANANA SUNDAE

2 tablespoons margarine
¼ cup packed brown sugar
1 tablespoon fresh lemon juice
⅛ teaspoon ground cinnamon
1 tablespoon water
4 ripe medium bananas, peeled, cut crosswise
  in half, then lengthwise in half
1 teaspoon vanilla extract
1 pint vanilla ice cream

In a large skillet, melt margarine over medium heat. Add sugar, lemon juice, cinnamon, and water. Stir until sugar begins to melt. Place bananas in single layer in skillet. Cook until slightly softened, about 1 minute per side, occasionally shaking skillet. Remove skillet from heat. Add vanilla extract. Mix without tearing bananas. Serve warm bananas with sauce over ice cream. Makes 4 servings.

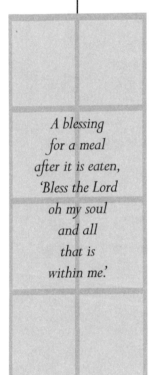

A blessing for a meal after it is eaten, 'Bless the Lord oh my soul and all that is within me.'

Fluffy Marshmallow Squares

¼ cup margarine
40 large marshmallows
5 cups crispy rice cereal
½ cup chocolate coated candy (frozen)
1 teaspoon butter

In a large saucepan over low heat, melt margarine. Add marshmallows, stirring constantly, until melted. Remove from heat. Quickly add cereal and chocolate coated candy, stirring until all pieces are evenly coated. Press mixture into buttered 9x13 inch baking pan with the back of a buttered spoon. Cut into squares for serving. Makes 8 to 10 servings.

Plain Ole Fudge

3 cups sugar
1½ cups milk
7 teaspoons cocoa
2 teaspoons butter
½ teaspoon vanilla extract
1 teaspoon butter

In a saucepan over medium heat, melt sugar, milk, and cocoa. Stir often. Cook until fudge makes a soft ball when dropped into cold water. Remove from heat. Add butter and vanilla. Beat until firm. Pour into buttered 9x13 inch glass pan. When hardened cut into squares. Makes 6 to 8 servings.

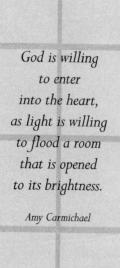

*God is willing
to enter
into the heart,
as light is willing
to flood a room
that is opened
to its brightness.*

Amy Carmichael

CREAMY CHOCOLATE FUDGE

3 cups sugar
¾ cup margarine
⅔ cup evaporated milk
2 cups chopped nuts
12 ounces semisweet chocolate chips
1 (7 ounce) jar marshmallow creme
1 teaspoon vanilla extract
1 teaspoon butter

In a large saucepan, combine sugar, margarine, and milk. Bring to the boiling point, stirring constantly to dissolve sugar. Cook, covered, for 2 to 3 minutes or until steam washed sugar crystals form on side of pan. Cook, uncovered, over medium heat for 5 minutes. Remove from heat. Add nuts, chocolate chips, marshmallow creme, and vanilla. Beat until mixture thickens and loses it's luster. Pour into buttered 9x13 inch dish. Let stand until firm. Cut into squares. Makes 10 to 12 servings.

PLAY 'N EAT PEANUT BUTTER BALLS

1 cup peanut butter
1 cup corn syrup
1¼ cups powdered milk
1¼ cups confectioners' sugar

In a medium bowl, combine all ingredients. Mix well. Shape mixture into small balls. Makes 4 servings.

If you can see the miracles in nature, you can have hope.

CORN FLAKE KOOKY-CANDY

1 (8 ounce) bag semi-sweet chocolate chips
1 tablespoon peanut butter
2 tablespoons melted paraffin
2 cups corn flakes

In a double boiler, combine all ingredients. Melt and mix together. Drop mixture by teaspoonfuls onto waxed paper. Cool. Makes 6 to 8 servings.

CHOCOLATEY PEANUT BUTTER

1 (16 ounce) jar creamy peanut butter
1 (16 ounce) box confectioners' sugar
½ pound margarine, melted
¾ cake paraffin
1 (12 ounce) bag chocolate chips

In a large bowl, combine peanut butter, confectioners' sugar, and margarine. Shape mixture into balls and refrigerate overnight. In a double boiler, melt paraffin and chocolate chips. Stick a toothpick in a peanut butter ball and dip in chocolate-paraffin mixture. Set on waxed paper to dry. Makes 10 to 12 servings.

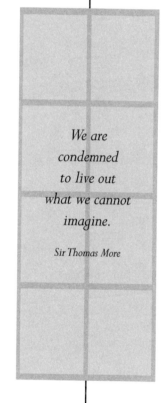

*We are
condemned
to live out
what we cannot
imagine.*

Sir Thomas More

CANDY-DIPPED PRETZELS

6 cups candy melts, assorted colors
12 large pretzel twists
Assorted decorative sprinkles

In a small saucepan, melt candy melts, do not mix colors. Dip half of each pretzel into candy melt allowing excess to drip off. Place on wax paper. Lightly sprinkle with assorted decorative sprinkles. Makes 10 to 12 servings.

GOLDEN STREETS PEANUT BRITTLE

2 cups sugar
1 cup corn syrup
½ cup cold water
2 cups peanuts, shelled
2 teaspoons soda
1 teaspoon vanilla
1 teaspoon vegetable oil

In a medium pan, combine sugar, syrup, and water. Mix well. Bring to a boil. Add peanuts. Cook until you hear the peanuts popping. Remove from heat and immediately add soda. Stir well. Add vanilla. While mixture is still foaming, pour mixture into greased 9x13 inch baking pan. Let cool and break into pieces. Makes 8 to 10 servings.

HEAVENLY ORANGE BALLS

1 cup margarine, melted
1 (6 ounce) can frozen orange juice
1 (16 ounce) box confectioners' sugar
½ cup finely pecans
1 (12 ounce) box vanilla wafers, crumbled
1 cup flaked coconut

In a large saucepan, combine margarine and orange juice. In a large bowl, combine sugar, pecans, and vanilla wafer crumbs. Mix well. Stir into orange juice mixture. Blend until smooth. Shape mixture into small balls and roll in coconut. Makes 16 to 18 servings.

Why is love necessary for a successful marriage? Because the pathway is strewn with many trials and troubles.

YUMMIES

2 sticks margarine
2 cups packed dark brown sugar
1 (16 ounce) box pitted dates, cut in small pieces
1¼ cups flaked coconut
2 cups chopped pecans
4 cups crisp rice cereal
1 cup confectioners' sugar

In a large saucepan, melt margarine and brown sugar. Add dates and coconut. Cook over medium heat for 6 minutes. Stir in pecans and rice cereal. Cool. Form in finger length rolls and roll in confectioners' sugar. Makes 10 to 12 servings.

NO-FAIL DIVINITY CANDY

3 cups sugar
½ cup corn syrup
⅔ cup water
2 egg whites
⅛ teaspoon salt
1 teaspoon vanilla
1 cup chopped pecans
½ cup whole pecans

In a large saucepan, boil sugar, corn syrup, and water until it forms a hard ball when dropped in water. In a large glass bowl, beat egg whites, salt, and vanilla for 3 minutes, or until fluffy. Slowly pour syrup into egg whites constantly beating. Continue beating until mixture passes the glossy stage. Add chopped nuts. Continue beating until mixture forms a peak when beater is raised. Immediately drop by spoonsfuls onto waxed paper. Place a whole pecan in the center of each piece. Allow candy to set until hard. Makes 10-12 servings.

There is so much bad in the best of us, and so much good in the worst of us, that we shouldn't talk about the rest of us.

Anonymous

CREAM CHEESE CANDY

1 (8 ounce) package cream cheese
1 (16 ounce) box confectioners' sugar
1½ cup chopped pecans or walnuts
1 teaspoon vanilla extract

In a double boiler, melt cream cheese. Combine in sugar, nuts, and vanilla extract. Mix well. Immediately drop mixture by spoonfuls onto wax paper. Makes 6 to 8 servings.

CANDIED MACADAMIA NUTS

1 (20 ounce) package white almond bark
2 cups whole Macadamia nuts, toasted
¾ cup coconut

In a double boiler, melt almond bark. Add nuts and coconut. Mix well. Pour mixture onto waxed paper. Refrigerate 30 minutes. Break into pieces. Makes 10 to 12 servings.

PECAN CARAMELS

2 cups sugar
1¾ cups dark Karo syrup
1 stick butter
2 (8 ounce) cartons whipping cream
1¼ cups chopped pecans

In a large saucepan, combine sugar, syrup, butter, and 1 carton whipping cream. Bring to a boil. Add second carton of cream. Cook until mixture forms a soft ball when dropped into cold water. Beat by hand for 5 minutes. Add pecans. Mix well. Pour onto a buttered baking sheet. Cut into pieces when cool. Makes 12 to 14 servings.

The devil often laughs when we work, but he trembles when we pray.

Corrie Ten Boom

Index

bread and rolls
(see also Biscuit, Cornbread and Muffins)

Apple Pancakes, 179

Apple Roly Poly, 170

Aunt Fay's Cinnamon Bread, 173

Busy Day Cinnamon Rolls, 189

Buttermilk Rolls, 188

Cheesy Brown 'n Serve Rolls, 187

Chewy Bread, 168

Cinnamon French Toast, 177

Cinnamon Raisin Coffee Rolls, 190

Cranberry Bread, 171

Crossed-up Dinner Rolls, 187

Easy Cinnamon Toast, 176

Eight To Ten Minute Rolls, 187

Family Favorite Banana Nut
Bread, 172

Family Fun Homemade Pretzels, 178

French Breakfast Puffs, 175

Fried Bread, 177

Fruit Bread, 169

Homemade Rolls, 186

Italian Garlic Bread, 167

Light and Fluffy Pancake Batter, 178

Nutty Cinnamon Ring, 190

Oatmeal Bread, 171

Oh Boy Waffles, 179

Orange Nut Bread, 173

Party Bread, 168

Poppy Seed Bread, 169

Poppy Seed Pull-Aparts, 176

Rise 'n Shine Coffee Bread, 174

Rolled Strawberry Treats, 175

Spicy Applesauce Bread, 170

The Best Banana Bread, 172

TLC Rolls, 186

Upside Down Caramel Rolls, 189

Vanilla Coffee Bread, 174

Yummy Sticky Rolls, 188

Breaded Snapper, 108

Broccoli and Pine Nuts Stir-Fry, 121

Broccoli Casserole, 157

Broccoli Cornbread, 161

Broccoli Salad, 52

Busy Day Cinnamon Rolls, 189

Butter and Sour Cream Biscuits, 183

Butter Pecan Fruit Cake, 201

Buttermilk Rolls, 188

C

Caesar Salad, 50

cakes and frostings

Apple Cream Cake, 199

Blueberry Cream Cake, 201

Butter Pecan Fruit Cake, 201

Cherry Cream Cake, 200

Cherry Pineapple Dump Cake, 202

Chocolate Angel Food Cake, 203

Chocolate Cheesecake Balls, 206

My favorite recipes

Order Form

Please send me _____ copies of **Home Made Blessings**

$19.95 (U.S.) tax included for each book $_____

Postage and handling @ $3.50 for each book $_____

TOTAL $_____

Enclose check payable to Diane Reasoner

To order with credit card fill in information below or order on line

☐ American Express ☐ Visa ☐ Discover ☐ MasterCard

Account # _____	MAIL TO: Gifts With Reason 3750 Colonial Trail Lilburn, GA 30047 1-770-921-9181
Expiration Date _____	
Signature _____	

Name _____

Address _____

City _____ State _____ Zip _____

Phone (day) _____ (night) _____

Order on line at www.giftswithreason.com

- -

Order Form

Please send me _____ copies of **Home Made Blessings**

$19.95 (U.S.) tax included for each book $_____

Postage and handling @ $3.50 for each book $_____

TOTAL $_____

Enclose check payable to Diane Reasoner

To order with credit card fill in information below or order on line

☐ American Express ☐ Visa ☐ Discover ☐ MasterCard

Account # _____	MAIL TO: Gifts With Reason 3750 Colonial Trail Lilburn, GA 30047 1-770-921-9181
Expiration Date _____	
Signature _____	

Name _____

Address _____

City _____ State _____ Zip _____

Phone (day) _____ (night) _____

Order on line at www.giftswithreason.com